Anxiety Disorders in Children

Rachel G. Klein
Cynthia G. Last

Volume 20.
Developmental Clinical Psychology and Psychiatry

SAGE PUBLICATIONS
The Publishers of Professional Social Science
Newbury Park   London   New Delhi

For information address:

SAGE Publications, Inc.
2111 West Hillcrest Drive
Newbury Park, California 91320

SAGE Publications Ltd.
28 Banner Street
London EC1Y 8QE
England

SAGE Publications Pvt. Ltd.
M-32 Market
Greater Kailash I
New Delhi 110 048 India

Printed in the United States of America

Library of Congress Cataloging-in-Publication Data

Klein, Rachel G.
   Anxiety disorders in children / by Rachel G. Klein and Cynthia G.
Last.
         p.   cm. — (Developmental clinical psychology and psychiatry
series ; 20)
   Includes bibliographical references.
   ISBN 0-8039-3220-0. — ISBN 0-8039-3221-9 (pbk.)
   1. Anxiety in children.   I. Last, Cynthia G.   II. Title.
III. Series: Developmental clinical psychology and psychiatry : v.
20.
RJ506.A58K54 1989
618.92'85223 — dc20   89-35234
                                                               CIP

FIRST PRINTING, 1989

Anxiety Disorders
in Children

About the series . . .

Series Editor: Alan E. Kazdin, Yale University

The Sage series in **Developmental Clinical Psychology and Psychiatry** is uniquely designed to serve several needs of the field. While the primary focus is on childhood psychopathology, the series also offers monographs prepared by experts in clinical child psychology, child psychiatry, child development, and related disciplines. The series draws upon multiple disciplines, as well as diverse views within a given discipline.

In this series . . .

CONTENTS

SERIES EDITOR'S INTRODUCTION

Interest in child development and adjustment is by no means new. Yet only recently has the study of children benefited from advances in both clinical and scientific research. Advances in the social and biological sciences, the emergence of disciplines and subdisciplines that focus exclusively on childhood and adolescence, and greater appreciation of the affect of such influences as the family, peers, and school have helped accelerate research on developmental psychopathology. Apart from interest in the study of child development and adjustment for its own sake, the need to address clinical problems of adulthood naturally draws one to investigate precursors in childhood and adolescence. Within a relatively brief period, the study of psychopathology among children and adolescents has proliferated considerably. Several different professional journals, annual book series, and handbooks devoted entirely to the study of children and adolescents and their adjustment document the proliferation of work in the field. Nevertheless, there is a paucity of resource material that presents information in an authoritative, systematic, and disseminable fashion. There is a need within the field to convey the latest developments and to represent different disciplines, approaches, and conceptual views to the topics of childhood and adolescent adjustment and maladjustment.

The Sage series on *Developmental Clinical Psychology and Psychiatry* is designed to serve uniquely several needs of the field. The series encompasses individual monographs prepared by experts in the fields of clinical child psychology, child psychiatry, child development, and related disciplines. The primary focus is on developmental psychopathology, which here refers broadly to the diagnosis, assessment, treatment, and prevention of problems that arise from infancy through adolescence. A working assumption of the series is that understanding, identifying, and treating problems of youth must draw on multiple disciplines and diverse views within a given discipline.

The task for individual contributors is to present the latest theory and research on various topics including specific types of dysfunction, diagnostic and treatment approaches, and special problem areas that affect adjustment. Core topics within clinical work are addressed by the series. Authors are asked to bridge potential theory, research, and clinical practice, and to outline the current status and future directions. The goals of the series and the tasks presented to individual contributors are demanding. We have been extremely fortunate in recruiting leaders in the fields who have been able to translate their recognized scholarship and expertise into highly readable works on contemporary topics. *Anxiety Disorders in Children,* by Drs. Rachel G. Klein and Cynthia Last, provides a concise yet comprehensive evaluation of anxiety disorders in children. The authors trace the conceptualizations of anxiety disorders among children in historical context as a backdrop for contemporary advances. They then examine current theory and research on diverse topics including etiology, risk factors, diagnosis, comorbidity, assessment, psychotherapeutic and pharmacological treatments, clinical course, and long-term outcome, among other topics. In all, the topics are woven with remarkable scholarship and with an informative array of case studies, laboratory investigations, and epidemiological and diagnostic research. Worth mentioning is the fact that the literature they integrate so well has advanced in no small measure from their own scientific contributions on anxiety. This book not only reports the latest work on anxiety disorders but also points to areas where significant questions remain.

—*Alan E. Kazdin, Ph.D.*

PREFACE

From epidemiological studies conducted with adults we now know that anxiety disorders are strikingly common in the general population. Furthermore, the onset of adult anxiety disorders occurs frequently in childhood or adolescence; therefore, it seems especially important and worthwhile to focus our attention on the anxiety disorders of childhood and adolescence. In this book we summarize recent work on this topic with an emphasis on work that has relied on the nomenclature established in *Diagnostic and Statistical Manual of Mental Disorders, Third Edition,* (DSM-III), which was the first diagnostic system to identify anxiety disorders with a childhood onset. We opted to include a chapter on the history of anxiety in children to outline the direction the field has taken over the years. It is clear that we are moving away from an interest in hypothetical psychological constructs to more empirically rooted views of childhood and adolescent anxiety. The changes in our understanding of psychopathology are certainly reflected here as well.

During the past 30 years there has been tremendous scientific activity in psychiatry, largely spurred by the discovery of psychoactive agents and family studies that supported the theory of genetic transmission of psychiatric disorders. Developmental psychology is influencing recent concepts of anxiety in early life as well. There has always been the hope that an understanding of normal developmental processes would enrich our knowledge of psychopathology. It is probably fair to say that if this hope has materialized at all, it is in the field of anxiety.

We do not claim to have provided a completely exhaustive review of the anxiety disorders in childhood and adolescence. We have covered several important areas that reflect the authors' interests. It certainly would have been pertinent to include the important work being done with animals, especially primates, and also to review psychophysiological correlates of anxiety. We opted to focus on human development only since the book is aimed at clinicians. We decided to forego the inclusion of psychophysiological measures at this time since most of the work has been done with adults and no satisfactory body of knowledge has appeared that is relevant to our current classification of childhood and adolescent anxiety disorders.

1

HISTORICAL OVERVIEW

Most of us have some fascination with the past and with the views held by our predecessors. In psychopathology, however, the past has more than intrinsic, entertaining appeal; it also has important practical implications because it affects views of mental illness, which in turn determine treatment practices. A brief historical overview of childhood anxiety theories is presented since it clarifies the foundations of current thought and practice.

In the long history of human interest in anxiety, children have largely been ignored. It was not until the 19th century that specific attention was given to children, and even then mostly as a means of providing a fuller understanding of adult psychopathology. It wasn't until the end of the 19th and beginning of the 20th century that children themselves became the object of concern regarding the development of anxiety and its pathological consequences.

EARLY FORMULATIONS

Kierkegaard, who put angst at the center of his conception of man's condition, was the first to examine the origins of anxiety in early development (Kierkegaard, 1944). The infant experiences a diffuse, objectless anxiety that Kierkegaard associated with a vague awareness of "possibility." It is only when he becomes conscious of himself, some time between ages 1 and 3, that the child begins to become aware of his "freedom" and the choices and conflicts it presents. With this awareness comes anxiety. Kierkegaard reinterpreted the Biblical story of Adam who knew good and evil when he ate the apple as a symbolic retelling of a universal developmental crisis.

AUTHORS' NOTE: We wish to acknowledge the major contribution by Andrew Kuhn, M.A., to this chapter.

Kierkegaard's psychiatrict contemporaries were far from addressing the crises of normal development. A few were just beginning to debate the existence of insanity among the young. As a rule, fearful children did not meet the criteria for "caseness" unless they suffered from "night terrors" *(pavor nocturnus)*.

In the United States Benjamin Rush declared in the early 1800s that madness in children was rare before puberty because of the instability of their brains (Rubinstein, 1948). There was less American literature than European literature on childhood anxiety before the turn of the 20th century. By then, the European psychiatry texts contained brief discussions of childhood mental disorders, albeit restricted to the most severe pathology.

Kraepelin's 1883 compendium initiated a widening of clinical scope (Walk, 1964). Kraepelin stressed the child's great impressionability and consequent tendency to mood swings, and specifically mentioned anxiety states as a disorder of later childhood. As a preventive measure, Kraepelin recommended avoiding academic overstrain. Subsequently the plight of the overburdened, neurasthenic schoolboy became a focus of concern and effort at reform. For the first time disturbances accompanied by anxiety in children who were clearly not "mad" were recognized, diagnosed, and seen as meriting intervention.

Soon after Kraepelin's work, the first full volume on childhood mental disorders was published, Emminghaus's 1887 *Psychic Disturbances of Children.* Emminghaus argued that childhood and adult mental diseases differed and should be distinguished (Harms, 1967). He spelled out a variety of psychological as well as organic causes of psychic abnormality, including fright, anxiety, and grief. (The current distinction between psychosis and neurosis had not been made yet, and Emminghaus referred to all childhood disorders as *psychosis,* a term then not equivalent to its meaning today.)

Emminghaus's book appears to be the first to outline specifically "psychoneurotic" disorders of childhood. Anxiety as such occupies a prominent place in his presentation of deviations from normal functioning. He described the syndrome as *neurasthenia cerebralis,* characterized by mental overstrain, withdrawal, oversensitivity, tearful apprehension, and psychosomatic symptoms. (This more elaborate description had clear parallels with Kraepelin's account of the overstrained student.) Emminghaus, like his contemporaries, saw neural exhaustion, parental severity, and over-ambitiousness for the child as the cause of the syndrome (Harms, 1967). With its methodical search of the literature and inquiry into etiology, symptoms, and course, Emminghaus's account appears to be the first identifiable description of a childhood anxiety disorder. Others soon followed. Also in 1887 Langdon Downe mentioned "the children intermediate between the idiot and the lunatic, children of neurotic parents who break down under any vital strain," (quoted in Walk, 1964). In 1895 Theodor Heller, a pupil of Wilhelm Wundt (one of the first experimental psychologists), founded a school in Vienna that accepted children with neurotic complaints as well as mental defectives. In 1904 he discussed "nervous conditions of childhood," of which anxious mood is a prominent feature.

When Charles Darwin's *Origin of Species* appeared in November, 1859, its first printing of 1,500 copies sold out in one day. It is accepted that Darwin revolutionized not only biology but Western people's conception of themselves. Because Darwinism forms much of the background of contemporary thought it may be difficult to recognize the immediacy and force of Darwin's work and his influence in fields like psychology. Darwin's biological materialism itself challenged psychology to take account of the biological sciences.

In 1872 Darwin argued that fear, like other emotions, is communicated by universally recognized facial and postural expressions that evolved from the pressure of natural selection. Darwin also drew a distinction between anxiety and depression in terms echoed in more recent clinical literature: "If we expect to suffer, we are anxious; if we have no hope of relief, we despair" (Darwin, 1965). He also saw emotions as signals that serve to form bonds and regulate social relationships. Darwin's important views were virtually ignored by many major psychological thinkers, with some notable exceptions such as Pavlov. Freud, who probably has been the single most influential theoretician of anxiety in human psychology, mentioned the survival value of the human capacity to experience anxiety. He did not, however, integrate evolutionary theory into his views of personality development. It is only recently that an evolutionary view has become critical to theories of anxiety.

FREUDIAN CONCEPTS

While others had observed manifestations of anxiety in patients and touched on aspects of its origins, functions, and dynamics, Freud was the first to integrate anxiety into a comprehensive theory of psychological development. His ideas about anxiety changed markedly over a

40-year span. As he stated, "the problem of anxiety is a nodal point at which the most various and important questions converge, a riddle whose solution would be bound to throw a flood of light upon our whole mental existence." While Freud's explorations of the problem of anxiety stemmed initially from observations of his adult patients, his later work identified the developmental roots of anxiety.

To follow Freud's thinking about anxiety it is useful to review briefly some salient features of his model of mental functioning, which is essentially the Freudian theory of psychoanalysis today. Two fundamental hypotheses of psychoanalysis are that *all* psychic processes are psychologically determined, never epiphenomenal or random, and that most psychic processes are unconscious (Brenner, 1974). From birth the psychic apparatus operates in such a way as to maximize pleasure and avoid pain (the pleasure principle). Psychological development is characterized by a more or less turbulent passage through stages in which instinctual and psychic gratification are focused successively on the infant's oral, anal, and genital zones. Initially the infant is aware only of his own imperious instinctual needs, and of the environment insofar as it satisfies or frustrates those needs. Gradually the infant acquires the capacity to delay gratification and to discriminate discrete objects in the environment.

Wishes of a sexual and/or aggressive nature are directed in early life first toward the mother figure, then both parents. In the course of development the child's mental structure and functions become differentiated. The ego mediates the conflicting demands of the instinctual id and the prohibitions of the parents that are eventually internalized as the superego. Conflict is thus an inevitable feature of mental life. The difference between normal and pathological conflict is of degree rather than kind.

Though the instinctual aims of childhood are renounced, they are never abandoned and continue to operate unconsciously. The healthy ego makes use of a variety of largely unconscious defenses to deflect and mitigate the expression of these infantile urges. Ideally, the ego finds acceptable indirect outlets for their gratification. The failure of the defenses, whether partial (as in neurosis) or more nearly total (as in psychosis), results in a psychopathological breakthrough of id derivatives. Infantile wishes find both symbolic expression and partial satisfaction in psychopathological symptoms.

The evolution of Freud's thought about anxiety has been traced in detail by many authors (e.g., May, 1950; Sulloway, 1979). In his first formulations Freud conceived of the problem exclusively in energic, neurophysiological terms. Initially he considered that *aktual* (or current) neurosis results when libido, the psychic concomitant of sexual energy, is not discharged through orgasm during coitus. Undischarged libido was considered to have neurotoxic effects and was experienced as anxiety. While Freud later reaffirmed that anxiety neurosis could be caused by specific sexual practices — a view not taken up in the subsequent psychoanalytic literature — his later formulations dealt with anxiety and the anxiety disorders as specifically psychological phenomena with psychological causes. This is not to say Freud denied that humans have an innate proclivity to experience anxiety. He noted that the capacity to fear had survival value for infants as it does for other organisms. His main interest, however, was to elucidate the operation of anxiety in the mind.

Freud postulated that anxiety results from an overwhelming influx of stimuli, resulting in an unpleasurable state of tension, which the person is unable to master or discharge effectively. Such stimuli may be either of external or internal origin. Freud reasoned that an infant is particularly liable to such "traumatic situations," having a relatively underdeveloped ego. Freud considered the birth trauma the prototypical experience of anxiety, (though unlike Rank he did not elaborate this theoretically or therapeutically).

Specific situations in the course of development are liable to give rise to traumatic anxiety. An experience of deprivation of food when an infant is hungry, for instance, would be traumatic owing to the infant's inability to master or channel the intensity of his or her internal drive stimuli. In this case, while a failure of the environment has clearly precipitated the traumatic situation, the anxiety itself is considered to have internal origins, in that it has the experience of the internal drives that overwhelms the infant's rudimentary ego. In Freud's conception, traumatic anxiety is most often brought on by stimuli with an internal origin.

In the course of development, the child learns to anticipate traumatic situations before they become fully developed. This anticipation triggers a mild (sub-traumatic) experience of anxiety, which "signals" the ego to take action to avert the danger. The acquisition of signal anxiety is an important developmental achievement.

Freud adumbrated typical "danger situations" met in the course of development. As the child matures, he or she is liable to fear first the loss of the object, then the loss of the object's love. Later, in the phallic-Oedipal phase, the child's genital sensations and ambivalent affectional strivings toward his or her parents become especially intense, the child fears suffering the loss of the penis, or, in the girl, some analogous genital injury. The more or less successful "dissolution" of the Oedipus complex results in the establishment of the superego. In its capacity to inflict punishment in the form of guilt and remorse, the superego itself may give rise to a "danger situation." All of the typical anxieties center on losses — of the mother, of love, of the penis, of approval, and finally of life. All are considered to persist throughout life; in neurotics, they are particularly intense and disruptive. The flexibility and resourcefulness of a person's ego in both its assertive and defensive aspects largely determine whether the anxiety inevitably suffered in life will reach pathological proportions or remain at tolerable and indeed useful levels.

Freud's *Analysis of a Phobia in a Five-Year-Old Boy* (1909), the first psychoanalytic case study of a child who was also an anxious child, illustrates many of these points. Carried out by proxy — Little Hans's father was an enthusiastic adherent of Freud's ideas — the study has been attacked as biased and based on hearsay, and more parsimoniously understood in terms of learning theory than psychodynamics (Wolpe & Rachman, 1960). Still, unless one assumes that Hans's father was extraordinarily inventive, the detailed account provides a rich portrayal of pathological anxiety in a child. It remains a thorough description of childhood separation anxiety disorder as currently defined.

Freud interpreted Hans's symptoms — fear of horses and of going out — as manifestations of anxieties stemming from Oedipal conflicts. Freud cited evidence that while Hans wanted to sleep with his mother and have his father out of the way, the boy suffered pangs of conscience and feared his father's retaliation (castration). Horses symbolized the castrating father; the phobia, by preventing Hans from going out, served to keep him home with his beloved mother. In his discussion of the case, Freud noted that phobias ("anxiety-hysterias"), in addition to being the most common of all psychoneurotic disorders, are those that appear earliest in life.

Anna Freud stressed that anxiety associated with the typical "danger situations" outlined by Sigmund Freud is inevitably experienced in the course of development. Age-adequate mastery of anxiety is thus a key task for the ego. Children who respond actively to anxiety by attempting to master it rationally, by changing external circumstances, or by counterattacking will be less likely to fall prey to neurotic disturbance than those who retreat from anxiety. While brief, temporary regression is a common and often harmless response to anxiety. Regression is pathological when it arrests or reverses the progress of development. Sustained regression is only one of the more easily identified maladaptive means of responding to anxiety. Children who cannot bear even moderate amounts of anxiety attempt "to deny and repress all external and internal dangers which are potential sources of anxiety; or to project internal dangers onto the external world, which makes the latter more frightening; or to retreat phobically from danger situations to avoid anxiety attacks" (Freud, 1965, p. 137).

Anna Freud's observations and treatment of children led her to stress the wide variability in normal development and the difficulty of knowing how seriously to take any given symptom or pattern of functioning in the swiftly changing child. Despite the difficulty, however, she recommended attempting to make diagnostic distinctions on the basis of the degree of conflict internalization and the type of anxiety experienced by the child.

She recognized three main variations. In early childhood it is normal for the child's ego to side with the id, in accordance with the pleasure principle, bringing the child into conflict with the environment. The persistence of such patterns in later childhood, or a regression to them, is considered to be aroused by the external world as fear of annihilation due to loss of the object (usually the mother), fear of loss of the object's love, fear of criticism and punishment by the object, and fear of castration. In such cases, Anna Freud maintained, environmental intervention may bring change relatively quickly, since the conflict has not yet been internalized; that is, it has not been built into the child's character. A greater degree of internalization has been reached by children who despite continued impulse discharge and conflict with the environment identify with parental figures and introject their authority as their superego. Their anxiety is manifested as fear of the superego, or guilt. Therapy with children whose conflicts have been internalized to this degree takes some time, but not an inordinate amount. A third type of conflict occurs when the child has achieved full structuralization; the anxiety aroused by conflicts between the structures "remains in the depth" (Freud, 1965, p. 133) and can be dealt with only in the course of a prolonged analysis.

NEO-FREUDIAN CONCEPTS OF ANXIETY

Despite his movement away from physiological models of explanation and toward a more "purely" psychological one, Freud's broadly organismic perspective had remained steeped in a conception of a man as a creature rooted in drive/defense conflicts. After Freud, psychological theory tended away from biologically based views toward those that stressed the importance of social factors (Erikson, 1950). As part of the de-emphasis on instinct, other psychodynamic theorists went much further than Anna Freud in shifting the analytic and developmental emphasis from id to ego. These changes affected the theory of anxiety, which increasingly came to be seen as developing from and finding characteristic expression in a matrix of social relationships.

The Neo-Freudians attached the highest importance to environmental influences in human development, whether healthy or pathological. They differed from Freud in what they took to be the origins of anxiety and the nature of anxiety.

Sullivan, for instance, discarded Freud's libido theory and "intrapsychic" emphasis to stress the role of culture, where the individual is considered to develop a sense of identity through his or her interactions with other people. In this view, anxiety arises as a result of experienced maternal disapproval rather than internal conflict. Anxiety is seen as an unavoidable consequence of social living; the individual's response may be relatively successful and growth-promoting (sublimation) or not (selective inattention). Unlike fear, anxiety is "exclusively human" and "preternaturally social" (Sullivan, 1956). Also, unlike fear, severe anxiety is not adaptive because it renders the individual helpless.

Horney, like Sullivan, viewed anxiety more in interpersonal than intrapsychic terms, but went further in turning Freud's theory on its head. Rather than seeing instinctual drives as basic to anxiety, she concluded that, to the extent that they were compulsive, the drives themselves were products of anxiety, aiming "primarily not at satisfaction but at safety; their compulsive character is due to the anxiety lurking behind them" (Horney, 1945, p. 13). Like Sullivan, she saw anxiety as developing in early life as a result of disturbed relationships between the child and his parents. She suggested that a child's ambivalence toward his or her parents that stemmed from concurrent dependency and hostility was a typical conflict leading to childhood anxiety.

Those holding Freudian views of childhood anxiety suggest individual psychotherapy as the treatment of choice in order to identify the nature of the conflict and enable the child to develop more constructive means of coping. Neo-Freudians' views also favor psychotherapy, but as an interactive social process that provides corrective experiences for the early interpersonal deficits. While attempts have been made to measure therapeutic effects and to compare psychotherapeutic treatment modalities, the studies have been methodologically flawed, and results have not been informative.

CONDITIONING AND LEARNING THEORISTS

Although the work of the learning theorists proceeded at the same time as that of the psychoanalysts, it represents a quite divergent view of human behavior, in this case, childhood anxiety. Pavlov's investigation of psychic salivation in dogs was in part stimulated by Darwin's extension of evolutionary concepts from animal morphology and taxonomy to animal behavior. In a famous 1921 experiment, Pavlov induced an anxiety "neurosis" in a dog by presenting it with an increasingly difficult and finally impossible stimulus discrimination problem (circle versus ellipse) (Pavlov, 1941). While the proximate cause of the neurosis was the dog's experience, further experiments revealed that dogs with different "personalities" responded differently under the same experimental conditions. Persuaded that these differences were genetically mediated, Pavlov embarked on research into the genetics of behavior in the 1930s.

Unlike his immediate intellectual heirs in America, notably John Watson, Pavlov never doubted the importance of constitutional, hereditary factors in the development of psychopathology. Watson argued that the concept of consciousness and the technique of introspection led psychology nowhere; the study of behavior was its proper and sufficient domain (Watson, 1924). Watson soon extended the argument to a radical rejection of the "nature" side of the "nature-nurture" controversy, claiming that he could condition any dozen babies from birth to become doctors, thieves, anything at all.

In a notorious experiment, Watson conditioned an 11-month-old boy, Albert, to fear a white rat by clanging two iron bars together behind him each time he reached toward the animal. In short order Watson had created what looked very like a rat phobia in Albert, which spread to a dog, a fur coat, and, mildly, a Santa Claus beard. Albert's parents abruptly terminated their son's participation in the experiment, denying Watson the opportunity to show the efficacy of his techniques for curing as well as causing phobias (Watson & Rayner, 1920). In 1924, however,

Jones used a potpourri of conditioning techniques — each of which has since been elaborated in theory and practice — to help a 3-year-old boy, Peter, overcome a similar fear of white furry creatures and objects. He joined three nonphobic children in a play group, to which a rabbit was briefly introduced each day (what Bandura later termed "modeling"). He was systematically exposed to the rabbit at decreasing distances, first in and then out of the cage (today known as "systematic desensitization"). With each approach toward the rabbit, Peter was rewarded with a favored snack (Skinner's "shaping"). In time, Peter was able to play comfortably with the animal. All related fears also disappeared, and on follow-up the improvement was maintained (Jones, 1924).

In 1939 Mowrer took up the problem of anxiety from the perspective of conditioning theory, arguing "that anxiety is a learned response, occurring to signals (conditioned stimuli) that are premonitory of (i.e., have in the past been followed by) situations of injury or pain (unconditioned stimuli)" (Mowrer, 1960). Like most behaviorists Mowrer considered fear and anxiety interchangeable terms. The reduction of fear, he argued, "may serve powerfully to reinforce behavior that brings about such a state of relief or security" (Mowrer, 1960).

The specific nature of the signal is of no particular significance. The principle of *equipotentiality* argues that only two factors matter: the temporal relationships between the conditioned and unconditioned stimuli and the frequency of their pairing. All unconditioned stimuli are equivalently likely to induce anxiety or fear. The strongest evidence for this view comes from the voluminous literature on animal experiments that have relied on conventional conditioning procedures to induce fear of previously neutral stimuli.

Eventually, however, doubts were raised that this model could account for all features of fear acquisition (Rachman, 1978). It proved difficult to condition a fear of some things — opera glasses, in one memorable experiment (Valentine, 1946) — but easy to do with others (spiders, snakes). Schacter, among others, observed that a significant proportion of phobic patients had had little or no direct exposure to the phobic object. Also, if phobias are responses to stimuli that have been followed by "situations of injury or pain," one would expect in a modern, urban society a much higher frequency of car phobias than of snake phobias, but such is not the case. Mowrer's model would also lead one to predict a high rate of fear acquisition under circumstances in which, in fact, it has been found to be low. The remarkable lack of phobias persisting in civilians subjected to nightly bombardments during World War II, for example, and the apparent failure of anxiety disorders occurrences to rise dramatically under such conditions, are not easily accounted for by simple conditioning principles.

The learning theories have had a major impact on the treatment of anxiety in childhood as well as adulthood. Multiple therapeutic strategies have evolved and have been investigated in systematic fashion, but mostly in adults (the work with children is summarized in Chapter 4). The therapies have the important merit of being definable; as a result they can be applied in fairly uniform fashion, thereby enabling replication. Scientifically, this feature is important. Each aspect of the treatments can be subjected to systematic evaluation and the overall approach can be streamlined or modified according to the demonstrated efficacy, or lack thereof, of specific components of the therapies. However, the fact that behavioral treatments can be tested experimentally should not be confused with demonstrated efficacy (as we note in Chapter 4, such evidence is lacking in childhood anxiety disorders).

Not all learning theorists have rejected hereditary influence in the development of pathological anxiety. Eysenck (1967) considered proneness to anxiety neurosis to be inherited. People who become anxious are born with nervous systems that have autonomic over-responsivity to noxious stimuli, and are characterized by an "excitation-inhibition imbalance" that causes them to become over-socialized introverts suffering excesses of guilt, shame, self-consciousness, and anxiety.

Prior to the availability of detailed neurobiological evidence, Eysenck hypothesized that the proneness to anxiety was mediated by the reticular activating system. Gray (1988) revised and adapted Eysenck's findings, arguing for a unified discrete subsystem in the cerebral nervous system that regulates human anxiety. This is not the place to retrace Gray's involved and highly technical argument, which is based on psychopharmacologic, behavioral, and genetic evidence. However, it is worth noting that he would define *anxiety disorders* as pathology resulting from a specific pattern of function in the subsystem regulating anxiety experiences. The pathology may have arisen "*either* as the result of trauma, infection, a major gene, and so on, *or* as the result of a cumulation of minor genes and/or environmental experiences" (Gray, 1988, p. 11). Though rich in its integration of data from a variety of fields, Gray's model does not provide an account of how this array of presumed causes leads to a common behavioral outcome.

ETHOLOGICAL REVIVAL

Darwin's hypothesis that emotions are innate, universal, and adaptive has already been noted. During the 1920s, experimental psychologists Landis (1924) and Sherman (1927) failed to confirm Darwin's assertions about the universal recognizability of facial expressions. Recent investigators have attacked their methodology, rehabilitated Darwin's arguments, performed cross-cultural and experimental studies, and attempted to develop a list of "fundamental" emotions. Izard's differential emotions theory posits that each fundamental emotion has characteristic neurophysiological, expressive, and phenomenological components (Izard, 1982). Fear is one of those fundamental emotions and a key component of anxiety.

Darwin's seminal idea that people, like other animals, are organized to optimize their chances for survival has borne a number of different lines of inquiry. The work of the ethologists Lorenz (1937) and Tinbergen (1958), who examined the social and especially the maternal behavior of animals, stimulated the exploration of analogous phenomena in higher apes and in humans. Harlow's observations of baby monkeys raised with mechanical surrogate mothers threw light on the importance for later development of mother-infant interaction, and the innate unlearned social behavioral tendencies of infants (Harlow & Harlow, 1965).

Applying the ethological concept of preparedness for learning to explain fear reactions, some authors have argued that as a result of natural selection we are biologically predisposed to learn to fear certain objects rather than others (Seligman, 1970; Klein, 1980). The great majority of phobias can be understood as having been sources of natural danger during human evolution, objects such as predators, the dark, and strange places. While the ethological theory may account for readiness to acquire fears of particular objects or situations, it does not address individual differences in fearfulness, or the mechanism for the acquisition of pathological anxiety.

RELATIONSHIP BETWEEN ANXIETY AND
ATTACHMENT IN DEVELOPMENT

The ethological perspective was explicitly extended to humans by Bowlby. He posited an innate proclivity in infants to perform communicative behaviors that elicit maternal emotions and protective behavior. For humans as for other mammals, attachment behaviors have survival value; for human infants, born less physically capable of maintaining contact with parents than most animals are, communicative behaviors acquire particular importance. For an infant to have to "learn" such behaviors from scratch would be highly ineffective, since the child would be unlikely to survive the first lesson. The attachment behavioral system, then, is seen as having been favored by natural selection to an unusual degree (Bowlby, 1969; 1973).

The attachment behavioral repertoire is not directly analogous to imprinting. It is not a rigid "fixed-action pattern" set off by an innate releasing mechanism that operates during a critical period, nor merely an array of specific behaviors. Although some, Bowlby for one, suggest that specific behavioral components that emerge very early in life — crying, smiling — may be thought of as fixed-action patterns, the attachment behavioral system is conceived instead as relatively flexible, goal-directed, and responsive to environmental changes, developing over time with considerable individual variation built into its biological programming (Ainsworth, 1978). The attachment system operates in a homeostatic manner to achieve the "set-goal" of a felt security. It can be "activated by the absence of or distance from an attachment figure, the arrival or departure of that figure, rejection by or unresponsiveness of that figure or others, or the advent of an unfamiliar situation or person. The system is affectively mediated and regulated, with anxiety functioning much like a signal.

In the course of development the behavioral system acquires important ideational components. As the child's nervous system matures, the child begins to develop "working models" or "cognitive maps" (Bowlby, 1969) comprised of internal representations of the attachment figure and the self; these models come to mediate attachment behavior in increasingly complex ways. The models are built on and modified by memories of experiences with the attachment figure, which lead to expectations about the accessibility and responsiveness of that figure.

During the first four to six months of life, the infant performs attachment behaviors somewhat indiscriminately, being incapable of consistently distinguishing its mother from others (especially visually). Subsequently the child begins to preferentially signal the attachment figure. The achievement of greater mobility brings an added capacity to seek attachment, and also an added impetus to do so (the ability to move away from mother necessitates efforts to find her again).

Prior to the elaboration of attachment theory, developmental psychologists had noted regularities in the manifestation of anxiety in children. By eight months, for most children, "stranger anxiety" has appeared. The child is now capable of distinguishing a familiar from an unfamiliar face, and may respond initially with fear to a stranger. It is during this stage that a specific attachment is believed to begin. Shortly after stranger anxiety begins, separation anxiety becomes evident. The child becomes distressed when left by the primary caretaker, and is not readily comforted by others.

The attachment system is thus bolstered by both positive and negative affects. Proximity to the mother is intrinsically pleasurable and therefore reinforcing, over and above the mother's role in satisfying and regulating the infant's drives. On this point attachment theory differs from both Freudian and learning theory models. Similarly, separation anxiety is viewed as being in the first instance not learned or derivative, but primary (Bowlby, 1969).

For the attachment behavioral system to have evolved, it must have been for the most part effective; that is, mothers must have responded to their infants' attachment efforts. Animal studies strongly suggest that, given a history of adequate mothering, mothers do indeed behave maternally. It is interesting to note, however, that for subhuman primate infants with "abusive" mechanical surrogate or natural mothers, attachment behaviors do not readily extinguish (Harlow & Harlow, 1965; 1971). This provides support for the contention that attachment is indeed preprogrammed, or "hard-wired." The tenacity of the child's tie even to an inadequate and/or abusive parent has also been borne out clinically, and is routinely weighed as a factor in the disposition of such cases.

Given that manifest distress at separation is normative in certain situations and/or at specific maturational stages, researchers and clinicians have not always found it easy to distinguish clearly pathological anxiety from the normal variant in children. Some of the clearest data have been afforded by observations of the most extreme and obviously traumatic separations. Robertson and Bowlby's studies of children separated from their parents and confined to sanatoria contributed to formulation of the issues later addressed by attachment theory (Robertson & Bowlby, 1952). They delineated three stages of response to separation: overt protest, despair, and "denial/detachment." Studies of monkeys provide support for the claim that the phenomena it describes are part of a biological inheritance; overt protest giving way to apparent "despair" has been observed reliably in response to separations of macaque infants from their mothers (Harlow & Suomi, 1974). (Note Darwin, quoted above, on the temporal relationship between anxiety and despair.)

The ethological view does not carry a single specific treatment implication. Since psychopathology might occur when the biological mechanisms controlling fearful affect become dysregulated, biological treatments such as drug therapies might seem to be germane to the ethological model. Such is not regularly the case. Bowlby remained a psychoanalyst, and subsequent attachment researchers as well have explained individual variations in "security of attachment" and pathological anxiety in terms of the child's early experiences with primary caregivers.

An animal study found that treatment with medication reduced distress at separation. In a laboratory study of infant monkeys undergoing separation, imipramine was found to reduce anxious behaviors and physiological reactions (Suomi, Seaman, Lewis, DeLizio, & McKinney, 1978). Although treatment efficacy has limited potential for confirming etiological models, positing a deranged biological system renders such treatments more likely to be considered.

FAMILY SYSTEM THEORY

General system theory began with a biological conception and proceeded to a focus on interactive relationships. At the first of the Macy conferences in 1942, representatives from anthropology, psychiatry, neurology, and electronics developed the idea of mutual causality. Focusing on structures and relationships of parts to parts and parts to wholes, they elaborated such properties of systems as openness, boundaries, use of feedback, and resistance to change (Barnes, 1985). (Some of these concepts have found their way into everyday language, and are used sometimes with only the most vague relationship to their original meanings.)

Applied to psychiatry, these ideas led to a new way of looking at family relationships. Close attention to patterns of interaction led to the hypothesis that families have characteristic maladaptive modes of communication and that the "identified patient" brought for treatment serves to maintain "homeostasis" of the particular family system.

Like all other psychological models, family system theory has seldom integrated its concepts into research strategies that would elucidate relationships between the phenomena it has identified as important and such diagnostic categories as the anxiety disorders. The main thrust of the theory has been to deflect professional treatment from the symptomatically anxious child to the family, which is viewed as the unit of dysfunction. Thus, family therapy is a sine qua non of the system's theory.

The anxious child acquires the mother's anxiety not by modeling, as some learning theorists would say, but through the type of communication he or she receives. This formulation has been applied especially to childhood separation anxiety (Eisenberg, 1958). The mother is believed to communicate to the child that indeed much is to be feared when he or she is away from her. Her goal in sending this message is to keep the child with her to assuage her own anxieties. When the child becomes symptomatically so anxious that he or she cannot separate, the mother has been fully effective in her communication. This view of childhood anxiety shares much with the system model of pathology.

DSM-III AND ITS SEQUELS

The personality theories have been influential in generating therapeutic innovations which, sadly, have all remained untested. However, they not only did not provide a taxonomy of pathological anxiety but they also implicitly devalued the notion of a diagnostic system. This rejection of a nosological approach to anxiety stems from viewing anxiety as a unitary psychological phenomenon with similar antecedents for the normal as well as the pathological forms, and from the notion that the same psychological mechanisms occur in all manifestations of anxiety (whether they be separation anxiety, social phobias, specific phobias, etc.).

Up to the advent of DSM-III (APA, 1980) the diagnostic manual, (DSM-II [APA, 1962]) reflected the above view, and a very mixed group of anxiety disorders were grouped under "Phobic Neurosis," which was applied to children and adults. DSM-III was truly innovative in eschewing presumed models of psychopathology in favor of a clinical, descriptive approach. (The childhood anxiety disorders are described in Chapter 2). No assumption is made regarding underlying causes. If the clinical phenomenology is sufficiently distinguishable, the syndrome becomes a separate diagnosis. It is rarely appreciated that this approach was necessitated by psychiatric diagnosis's lack of reliability. By providing clinical descriptions and a common language, the

DSM-III has done much to foster communication and a real chance at learning more about the correlates, antecedents, treatment, and natural history of childhood anxiety disorders — what progress in psychopathology is made of. We can say that we have turned a historical corner in a way heretofore impossible. The notion of a unitary, discrete "anxiety" system, be it psychological or biological, is unlikely to be accurate. The empirical investigation of the various anxiety disorders will provide an opportunity for examining the issue critically and contribute to a better understanding of the nature of anxiety.

SUMMARY

Historically, interest in childhood anxiety came into its own in the early 20th century with Freud's work. Freudian theory was influential in emphasizing the role of unconscious psychological processes in determining anxious symptomatology. The neo-Freudians modified the early psychoanalytic views by de-emphasizing the role of unconscious drives in anxiety, and stressing instead the importance of early social, especially parent-child, relationships.

The discovery of conditioning mechanisms by Pavlov was instrumental in shaping a new model of childhood anxiety, one predicated on association learning. Considerable diversity in learning theories developed. Some put exclusive emphasis on conditioning paradigms, whereas others accepted the notion of proneness to anxiety as an unlearned characteristic. The latter view harks back to Darwin's contribution concerning the adaptive role of emotions in behavior. An extension of evolutionary models has led recently to the notion that there are innate biological processes that facilitate the acquisition of certain fears and anxieties. According to ethological models, an infant's innate tendency to seek close contact with the caregiver is activated by an experience of anxiety that, in the first instance, is an adaptive, unlearned response.

DSM-III represents the first attempt to provide a classification of childhood anxiety disorder. Its merit is still in question, although the classification has made systematic examination of childhood anxiety disorders possible for the first time.

2

DIAGNOSIS AND CLASSIFICATION

During the 1970s and 1980s we witnessed a dramatic increase in attention paid to adult anxiety disorders, but it only is very recently that similar attention has been paid to the childhood anxiety disorders. It is probable that the major classification changes that appeared in the third edition of the *Diagnostic and Statistical Manual of Mental Disorders* (DSM-III) in 1980 are responsible, at least in part, for spurring interest in anxious children and adolescents. At that time a new diagnostic category was introduced that specifically focused on anxiety disorders that usually first arise during childhood or adolescence, Anxiety Disorders of Childhood or Adolescence. This category included three specific disorders — separation anxiety disorder, avoidant disorder, and overanxious disorder — only one of which (overanxious reaction) appeared in previous versions of the DSM.

Traditionally, adult models of psychopathology have served as templates for classifying and understanding psychopathology in children. To some extent this holds true for the DSM-III and the more recent DSM-III-R (American Psychiatric Association, 1987) classification scheme for anxiety disorders, in that most of the "adult" anxiety diagnoses can be and often are applied to children and adolescents (i.e., phobic disorder, obsessive-compulsive disorder, panic disorder, post-traumatic stress disorder, generalized anxiety disorder). The diagnostic criteria for these disorders contain very few modifiers for developmental differences that may occur. While the anxiety diagnoses appearing in the childhood section (Anxiety Disorders of Childhood or Adolescence) appear to attend to developmental issues to a greater degree, empirical investigations are needed to determine whether each of the disorders and their criteria best reflect the phenomenology of maladaptive anxiety in young children and adolescents.

DSM CLASSIFICATION

While anxiety is considered to be the central feature for the Anxiety Disorders of Childhood or Adolescence, it is focused on specific situations in separation anxiety and avoidant disorders, and generalized to a variety of situations in overanxious disorder.

The hallmark of *separation anxiety disorder* is excessive anxiety concerning separation from major attachment figures, for example, parents, home, or other familiar surroundings. In DSM-III, there are nine specific criteria for the diagnosis; at least three must be met:

1. Unrealistic worry about possible harm befalling major attachment figures or fear that they will leave and not return.
2. Unrealistic worry that an untoward calamitous event will separate the child from a major attachment figure (e.g., the child will be lost, kidnapped, killed, or be the victim of an accident).
3. Persistent reluctance or refusal to go to school in order to stay with major attachment figures or at home.
4. Persistent reluctance or refusal to go to sleep without being next to a major attachment figure or to go to sleep away from home.
5. Persistent avoidance of being alone in the home or emotionally upset if unable to follow the major attachment figure around the home.
6. Repeated nightmares involving the theme of separation.
7. Complaints of physical symptoms on school days (e.g., stomachaches, headaches, nausea, vomiting).
8. Signs of excessive distress on separation or when anticipating separation from major attachment figures (e.g., temper tantrums or crying, pleading with parents not to leave).
9. Social withdrawal, apathy, sadness, or difficulty concentrating on work or play when not with a major attachment figure.

In addition to displaying three of these symptoms, the disturbance must be at least two weeks in duration. Further, DSM-III notes that if the child is 18 years or older, he or she does not meet the criteria for agoraphobia.

It should be noted that in DSM-III-R a few changes emerged for the criteria for this diagnosis. Criterion 8 has been divided into two separate criteria: One is excessive distress *when anticipating* separation, the other is excessive distress *during* separation. In addition, criteria 9 has been deleted from the list of symptoms. Finally, the onset of the disorder must be before 18 years of age.

In *avoidant disorder of childhood or adolescence,* anxiety is focused on contact with unfamiliar persons, resulting in persistent avoidance or shrinking from both adults and peers. More specifically, both DSM-III and DSM-III-R include three criteria: (1) persistent and excessive shrinking from contact with strangers, (2) desire for affection/acceptance and generally warm and satisfying relations with family members and other familiar figures, and (3) avoidant behavior sufficiently severe to interfere with social functioning and peer relationships. In addition to meeting all three of these criteria, the child must be at least 2½ years old, and must not meet criteria for Avoidant Personality Disorder. Finally, the duration of the disturbance must be for at least six months.

Contrasting the two diagnostic categories described above, the essential feature of *overanxious disorder* is excessive worry and fearful behavior that is not limited to a specific situation or object. According to both DSM-III and DSM-III-R, the child must meet four of the following seven criteria:

1. Unrealistic worry about future events.
2. Preoccupation with the appropriateness of the individual's behavior in the past.
3. Overconcern about competence in a variety of areas (e.g., academic, athletic, social).
4. Excessive need for reassurance about a variety of worries.
5. Somatic complaints, such as headaches or stomachaches, for which no physical basis can be established.
6. Marked self-consciousness or susceptibility to embarrassment or humiliation.
7. Marked feelings of tension or inability to relax.

The symptoms must have persisted for at least six months. Further, if the child is 18 years or older, he or she does not meet criteria for generalized anxiety disorder. In both versions of the manual the disturbance cannot be due to another mental disorder, such as separation anxiety disorder, avoidant disorder, phobic disorder, obsessive/compulsive disorder, depressive disorders, schizophrenia, or pervasive developmental disorder.

Other anxiety diagnoses that may be applied to children and adolescents as well as adults are included in DSM-III-R: simple phobia, social phobia (including generalized type), panic disorder with and without agoraphobia, obsessive/compulsive disorder, posttraumatic stress disorder, and generalized anxiety disorder. In simple and social phobics, fear and avoidance are associated with a specific object or situation with the exclusion of separation (separation anxiety disorder) or contact with strangers (avoidant disorder). The essential feature of panic disorder involves panic attacks that occur spontaneously, and not on exposure to a particular phobic stimulus life-threatening situation, or during physical exertion. If in addition to panic attacks there is avoidance of certain situations, such as crowds, theatres, public conveyances, from which escape may be difficult, panic disorder with agoraphobia is the appropriate diagnosis. In obsessive-compulsive disorder, obsessions or compulsions that are time-consuming, impairing, and/or cause marked distress prevail. Posttraumatic stress disorder is an anxiety reaction that occurs following exposure to a traumatic event. Typically, the disorder is characterized by the distressing reexperience of that event. Finally, in generalized anxiety disorder, unrealistic or excessive worry is accompanied by multiple signs of motor tension, autonomic hyperactivity, and vigilance and scanning.

During the past three years, Last and colleagues have evaluated over 250 children and adolescents referred for anxiety problems at their Child and Adolescent Anxiety Disorder Clinic. Data from the clinic has shown separation anxiety disorder and overanxious disorder to be the most common anxiety disorders evaluated at the outpatient facility. Avoidant disorder also has been observed frequently at the clinic, although much less often than separation anxiety or overanxious disorders. Only a handful of children and adolescents have received the diagnosis of panic disorder (with or without agoraphobia), obsessive-compulsive disorder, or posttraumatic stress disorder. Interestingly, not one youngster to date has met criteria for generalized anxiety disorder. While a large number of children with phobic disorders associated with school avoidance have been evaluated at the clinic, youngsters presenting with primary complaints for other types of phobias have been relatively rare.

In the remainder of this chapter, we primarily will direct attention to the three Anxiety Disorders of Childhood or Adolescence: separation anxiety disorder, overanxious disorder, and avoidant disorder. We also briefly will discuss obsessive-compulsive disorder because of the substantive efforts that have been devoted to the treatment of this condition (see Chapter 4).

Separation Anxiety Disorder

Children with separation anxiety disorder often are referred to a mental health setting by their parents who are distressed by their child's reluctance or inability to be separated from them. In most cases, the child has difficulty separating from his or her mother. However, there are instances in which the child is fearful of being away from the father, siblings, or other significant individuals to whom the child is attached. In young children with this disorder, clinging behavior is common. On presentation at a mental health setting, the child may refuse to have the parent or parents leave him or her to meet with the clinician. When anticipating separation, young children may throw a tantrum, cry, or scream. At the extreme end of this type of behavior, the child may threaten suicide (e.g., "If you leave me, I'm going to throw myself out the window") or make suicidal gestures.

In clinic attendees, school reluctance or refusal is a common feature of the disorder, although not required by DSM-III or DSM-III-R for a diagnosis. Last, Francis, Hersen, Kazdin, and Strauss (1987) have noted that approximately three-quarters of children who meet criteria for the diagnosis of separation anxiety disorder show school reluctance or avoidance among clinic referrals. Concomitant with school reluctance/avoidance are somatic complaints, where the child complains of stomachaches or headaches or sometimes general malaise ("I don't feel good") prior to going to school. Somatic complaints also can occur in the context of other situations where separation is anticipated. At times, the child has such complaints while in school, and is sent home as a result. Although recent evidence suggests that separation anxiety disorder is rarer in adolescents than children (see Last, Hersen, Kazdin, Finkelstein, & Strauss, 1987), adolescents with the disorder who come for treatment almost always present with school reluctance/avoidance and somatic complaints (Francis, Last, & Strauss, 1988).

Many younger children with separation anxiety "shadow" the individual from whom they are afraid to be separated. More specifically, they will follow the parent around the house, always being in close proximity (i.e., two steps behind). During middle childhood and adolescence, these children often are reluctant or refuse to sleep away from home, for example, at a friend's house or to go away to sleep-away camp. They are typically fearful of entering unfamiliar situations. These concerns are best understood as maintaining the child's strong wish to have ready access to the mother or home. Repeated nightmares with separation themes (i.e., being kidnapped, killed, the death of a parent, etc.) sometime are reported in younger children with the disorder; nightmares very rarely are reported by adolescents with the disorder (Francis, Last, & Strauss, 1988). However, concerns about death and dying are not unusual among children and adolescents.

Worrying that focuses on the theme of separation is common to both children and adolescents with separation anxiety disorder. These worries may take the form of fears of getting kidnapped, being in an accident, getting killed, or the death of a major attachment figure. The child may worry about something happening to him- or herself, or the worries may be focused on what will happen to the parent. In many instances, both types of worries exist. It is quite common for these youngsters to refuse to be alone in the home, even when of an age where such behavior is expected and usual. In prepubertal children with the disorder, sadness, apathy, or difficulty concentrating may be experienced when the child is separated from his or her parent.

Recent evidence suggests that children with separation anxiety disorder often present with specific fears in addition to their separation anxiety, such as of the dark, ghosts, bumblebees, and so on, which may or may not be of phobic proportion (Last, Francis, & Strauss, in press). Approximately one-third of children with the disorder will show a concurrent overanxious disorder that almost always is secondary to a primary separation anxiety disorder (Last, Hersen, Kazdin, Finkelstein, & Strauss, 1987). Although the separation anxiety disorder, in such cases, typically is the presenting problem and the one that requires immediate intervention, it is not uncommon for the overanxious disorder to have preceded the onset of the separation anxiety disorder. It should be noted that children with separation anxiety usually do not have significant interpersonal difficulties. Generally such children are well liked by their peers and reasonably skilled socially.

Separation anxiety may have an acute or chronic onset. The onset often occurs after a major stressor, such as moving to a new neighborhood and a new school, the death of a family member, or illness of a relative. The onset of the disorder also has been noted to occur following prolonged vacations from school, such as after Christmas or summer vacation. Sometimes the disorder develops after a physical illness where despite evidence that the illness no longer exists, the child will continue to complain of the symptoms in an attempt to avoid separating from mother or home. It also has been noted that at certain developmental transitions, the incidence of the disorder increases, such as entry into elementary school or the transition between elementary school and junior high school. There is little data on the course of the disorder although it appears that, without intervention, it may wax and wane according to life stressors and developmental transitions. The literature pertaining to outcome is reviewed in Chapter 6. It is not uncommon for a child who presents with the disorder at 10, 11, or 12 years of age to have a history of problems on entering kindergarten or first grade. Currently, we are conducting follow-up studies of these children to determine more specifically the course and prognosis.

School Phobias Due to Simple and Social Phobic Disorders

By contrast to children with separation anxiety disorder, some children with phobias of school show fear and avoidance that is relatively well circumscribed (Last, Francis, Hersen, Kazdin, & Strauss, 1987; Last, Francis, & Strauss, in press). In other words, the phobic child will be fearful and avoid school alone, while the separation anxious child will be fearful and avoid a host of situations that are related to the theme of separation. The child with a circumscribed school phobia will be fearful of some aspect of the school environment. The nature of the fear can be either due to a simple phobia (for example, an excessive and/or irrational fear of being physically harmed by other children) or to a social phobic disorder (for example, an excessive and/or irrational fear of being criticized, ridiculed, or teased by teachers or other students). In distinguishing separation anxiety disorder from other phobic disorders of school, it is often helpful to inquire as to where the child is when not in school. Separation anxious children remain at home and/or in the presence of a major attachment figure when refusing school. In contrast, children with a phobia of school usually will be equally comfortable in any setting other than the school environment, not being limited to being at home or with mother.

Last, Francis, Hersen, Kazdin, and Strauss (1987) compared the clinical and associated features of separation anxiety disorder and phobic disorders of school in a clinic sample of children who met DSM-III criteria for the disorders. Analysis of demographic variables suggests that children with separation anxiety disorder and school phobia may represent two distinct populations. Children with separation anxiety disorder were more often prepubertal, and from families of lower socioeconomic status, while children with school phobia not due to separation concerns tend to be more often male, postpubertal, and from higher socioeconomic backgrounds. It should be noted that previous studies with school phobic children, which did not employ DSM-III criteria or distinguish children with separation anxiety from those with phobic disorders, have produced inconsistent demographic characteristics results (see review by Trueman, 1984).

Last, Francis, Hersen, Kazdin, and Strauss (1987) also found that children with overall separation anxiety disorder were more likely than children with school phobia to receive an additional DSM-III diagnosis. Indeed, virtually all of the children with separation anxiety disorder (92%) met criteria for at least one concurrent disorder, compared to 63% of the school phobia group. This difference suggests that children with separation anxiety disorder are more severely disturbed than children with school phobic disorder because they almost always manifest sufficient additional psychopathology to warrant a second diagnosis.

Overanxious Disorder

The hallmark of overanxious disorder is unrealistic worry about future events. In a study by Last and colleagues, 95% of children with overanxious disorder presented with this specific diagnostic clinical criterion (Strauss, Lease, Last, & Francis, 1988). In addition to worrying about future events, results indicated that it is quite common for children with this disorder to have unrealistic worries about the appropriateness of their behavior in the past. This was particularly true for adolescents, who almost always (90%) showed this problem. This second observation suggests that, as defined, overanxious disorder encompasses anxiety concerning social behavior.

Excessive and/or unrealistic concerns about competence is characteristic of overanxious children. They have been noted to be perfectionistic, wanting to excel in multiple performance areas, for example, academic performance, social interaction, sports, and so on. As in separation anxiety disorder, somatic complaints are common. However, in the case of overanxious disorder, the somatic complaints are not linked to any particular situation but rather appear to occur "spontaneously" or when the child is "tense." Somatic complaints often take the form of headaches, stomachaches, back pains, or a general feeling of malaise. These children tend to be markedly self-conscious and usually have difficulty speaking out loud in a group setting, such as at school. They also may be embarrassed when other people talk about them, even if the comments are of a positive nature. Because of their excessive worries and insecurities, children and adolescents with overanxious disorder often excessively and repeatedly seek reassurance from significant others. The reassurance-seeking behavior can be in relationship to their academic performance, social interaction, competence at sports or other hobbies or activities, and appearance. Finally, generalized tension and an inability to relax are characteristic. The tension may be expressed as "nervous habits," such as nail biting, foot tapping, hair pulling, and fidgeting.

The clinical content of the disorder is mixed, and many children with the disorder exhibit symptoms of generalized social anxiety. According to DSM-III-R, overanxious disorder should be diagnosed only in cases where the symptoms are not limited in content to another Axis I disorder; thus, if worries and concerns are *solely* related to social anxiety, a diagnosis of generalized social phobia should be considered, rather than overanxious disorder. However, it should be noted that many children with overanxious disorder exhibit specific, circumscribed social phobias (i.e., public speaking) in addition to their overanxious disorder (OAD) symptomatology; in these cases, it may be best to diagnose both conditions simultaneously.

On presentation at a mental health setting, parents of overanxious children often will state something of this nature: "My child is a worry wart and a nervous wreck." Because these children are usually quiet and well-behaved, it is unusual for school personnel to be the referral source for this type of anxiety disorder. More often, it is the child or the parents who identify this problem and seek help.

It is not uncommon among referred children for school phobia to occur as a complication of overanxious disorder. Three of the hallmarks of overanxious disorder include worrying, overconcern about competence, and marked self-consciousness. Children who show these symptoms of overanxious disorder may exhibit school reluctance or refusal in an attempt to avoid confronting anxiety-eliciting situations in the school environment. School avoidance is not a criterion for overanxious disorder, and it is not clear whether an additional diagnosis of a phobic disorder should be assigned in such cases.

In addition to school avoidance, it is not uncommon to see these children avoid engaging in other age-appropriate activities in which there are demands for performance, for example, sports, musical instruments, and so on. Obsessional self-doubt is sometimes observed in children with overanxious disorder, which can serve to exacerbate their worries about the future and past. On presentation, some children with overanxious disorder will appear as "little adults," that is, they will act and appear older than their chronological age. Approximately one-third of children seen in the clinic with the disorder met DSM-III criteria for a concurrent major depression (Last, Hersen, Kazdin, Finkelstein, & Strauss, 1987).

In contrast to separation anxiety disorder, overanxious disorder appears to be a more chronic (as opposed to episodic) disorder. On presentation at a mental health setting, it is typical for these children to have had a several-year history of the disorder without remission. Although the disorder does not appear to remit spontaneously, it may be exacerbated during times of intense stress or developmental transitions. The outcome or prognosis of the disorder is unknown at this time, and currently is being investigated in a prospective, longitudinal study by Last and colleagues.

Avoidant Disorder

In avoidant disorder, the child is excessively fearful about being around unfamiliar people. In most instances, the unfamiliar people include both children and adults, although cases where the child is more fearful around one or the other is not uncommon. This fear leads to avoidance behavior where the youngster is extremely reluctant to enter situations where there is someone he or she does not know. Children of this type generally are warm and loving with family and other people whom they know well. Avoidant disorder children should be distinguished from children who are "slow to warm up," for children with avoidant disorder virtually never "warm up."

Avoidant disorder can be apparent from the child's verbal and physical behavior during a psychiatric interview. In extreme cases, children may refuse to speak at all or crouch behind a piece of furniture. However, this reticence during examinations is not exclusive to them and can occur in other anxiety disorders. Avoidant disorder, in contrast to overanxious disorder, often is brought to mental health attention by school personnel. The children's discomfort in the school setting is most apparent to the teachers who observe them on a daily basis. Children with avoidant disorder typically have few or no friends since their ability to interact with new acquaintances is severely limited.

Children with avoidant disorder usually are very unassertive and lack self-confidence. In adolescence, normal heterosocial and heterosexual activities are avoided. Last and colleagues suggested that avoidant disorder rarely occurs alone (Francis, Last, & Strauss, 1988). In almost all cases, the child will have an additional concurrent anxiety disorder, in many cases, overanxious disorder.

As in overanxious disorder, children and adolescents with avoidant disorder usually have a long history of difficulties that do not appear to remit spontaneously. The avoidant behavior may exacerbate when the child is under sufficient stress or during significant developmental transitions. Without intervention, the problematic behaviors may proceed into college years. Sometimes the forced social exposure that occurs in college years is sufficient to remedy the condition. Although no data currently are available on the prognosis of the disorder, Last and colleagues currently are following these children prospectively.

Children with avoidant disorder by definition show impairment in their social interactions with peers and adults. The clinical features of avoidant disorder overlap to some extent with generalized social phobic disorders, and the distinctness of the two disorders requires specification.

No data currently are available on the prevalence or sociodemographic characteristics of separation anxiety disorder, overanxious disorder, and avoidant disorder in the general population. However, data are available on each of the three disorders from Last and colleagues' outpatient child and adolescent anxiety disorder clinic (Francis, Last, & Strauss, 1988; Last, Hersen, Kazdin, Finkelstein, & Strauss, 1987).

Separation anxiety disorder is one of the most common anxiety disorders evaluated at the clinic. Out of the first 91 children evaluated at the clinic, 47% (n = 43) met DSM-III criteria for separation anxiety disorder. Further examination of these children indicated that the vast majority are under the age of 13 (91%), with the mean age being 9.1 years. The sex distribution of the disorder was roughly equivalent for boys and girls. Finally, it should be noted that in the Pittsburgh clinic 75% of these children came from families of low socioeconomic status (Hollingshead ratings of 4 or 5), which is in contrast to other anxiety disorders seen at the clinic (i.e., overanxious disorder, school phobia).

Clinic data also suggests that overanxious disorder is as common as separation anxiety disorder, with 52% (n = 47) of the initial patient sample meeting DSM-III criteria for the disorder. However, in approximately one-half of these patients, overanxious disorder was concurrent with and secondary to a primary separation anxiety disorder. In contrast to separation anxiety disorder, children with overanxious disorder usually were over the age of 13 (69%), with the mean age being 13.4 years. The disorder was equally common in boys and girls in this patient sample. All of the cases evaluated during the 18-month period were Caucasian. In contrast to the separation anxious children, the majority of overanxious children (80%) came from families of middle to high socioeconomic status (Hollingshead ratings of 1, 2, or 3).

Preliminary data generated from Last and colleagues (Francis, Last, & Strauss, 1988) suggest that avoidant disorder is rarer that separation anxiety or overanxious disorders, at least among youngsters clinically referred for an anxiety disorder. Over a 24-month period, they collected information on 22 children with this disorder. The data suggest that avoidant disorder can occur at any age, with a mean age of 12.7 and equal incidence below and above 13 years of age. Females were over-represented (73%), as well as Caucasians (94%). Socioeconomic status was equally divided between upper and lower stratas, unlike separation anxiety and overanxious disorders.

Obsessive-Compulsive Disorder

Obsessive-compulsive disorder occurs more often to males compared with other anxiety disorders especially among the younger patients. This gender ratio, which had been noted in several clinical reports (Adams, 1973; Judd, 1965; Hollingsworth et al., 1980), was documented in the largest sample studied to date (N=70), 67% of which were male (Swedo & Rapoport, 1989). Furthermore, age of onset was negatively correlated with being male: 83% of the adolescents who had an onset before the age of 8 were male.

The disproportionate rate of affected males in the cases with very early onset suggests that perhaps males with early onsets have a different or more severe disorder than females or than males with later onsets. There are no confirmatory data for this proposition. On the whole, males and females have not been found to differ from females on indices of cognitive impairment (Keller, 1989) or other clinical features.

The content of the obsessions and compulsions among adolescents have not been found to differ from those characteristic of the adult disorder as defined in DSM-III-R. The obsessions of children and adolescents typically revolve around concerns about harmful events, death, and contamination. Compulsions involve checking and washing rituals, counting, and rigid ordering (Swedo & Rapoport, 1989).

Obsessive-compulsive disorder has been linked to Gilles de la Tourette disorder, a condition that always has a childhood onset (APA, 1987). Family studies of Gilles de la Tourette have found an excess of obsessive-compulsive disorder in the relatives and it is argued that the two conditions represent a spectrum of pathology of a single underlying genetically transmitted disorder (Pauls et al., 1986). If the two conditions are genetically linked, one would also expect them to have high comorbidity. Contrary to this hypothesis, Tourette disorder was not observed in a single case of obsessive-compulsive disorder by Swedo and Rapoport (1989).

COMORBIDITY OF CHILDHOOD
ANXIETY DISORDERS AND DEPRESSION

Research by Last and colleagues found that approximately one-third of 22 children who presented with separation anxiety disorder showed a coexisting major depression (Last, Hersen, Kazdin, Finkelstein, & Strauss, 1987). In these cases, the depressive disorder almost always antedated the onset of the separation anxiety disorder by several months. It was rare for such patients to have serious suicidal symptomatology; however, sometimes children made suicidal threats in an attempt to avoid or escape a dreaded separation situation.

In the same study (Last, Hersen, Kazdin, Finkelstein, & Strauss, 1987), the rate of depressive disorder among 26 children with overanxious disorder reached 42%. These findings suggest very high comorbidity of separation and overanxious disorders with major depression. Overall, a rate of 28% of depression in children referred to an anxiety clinic is reported by Strauss, Last, Hersen, and Kazdin (1988). Those with depression were older, more frequently Caucasian, and more often had multiple anxiety disorders compared with patients with pure anxiety disorders.

Other investigators also have examined the co-occurrence of depression in anxiety disorders, but the above study is the only one to report on specific anxiety disorders, applying uniform DSM-III criteria. In a small sample of 16 school refusers with an anxiety disorder, 13 (81%) were considered to have a depressive disorder as well (Bernstein & Garfinkel, 1986). The combination of the two was the rule, with pure form of either anxiety or depression being the exception.

Hershberg and colleagues studied over 100 children and adolescents referred for treatment, and identified 28 who met DSM-III diagnoses for depressive disorders, and 14 for anxiety disorders (Hershberg, Carlson, Cantwell, & Strober, 1982). Many of the depressed children had anxiety symptoms. Similarly, close to 30% of those with a primary anxiety disorder were judged to have depressive symptoms, but none was diagnosed as depressed.

Kolvin, Berney, and Bhate (1984) report that 45% of 51 cases of school phobia had significant depression. However, the definition of depression was very liberal. It required a sustained unhappy mood with only one other symptom from the following: appearance of gloom or tearfulness, lack of usual energy, feeling hopeless or that life is not worth living. This definition of depression is much less stringent from the DSM-III-R, which requires depressed mood or loss of interest or pleasure in addition to five other symptoms.

Comorbidity between obsessive-compulsive disorder and other psychiatric conditions has been noted by Swedo and Rapoport (1989). Among adolescents with obsessive-compulsive disorder, other anxiety disorders were frequent, occurring in about one-third of the cases. Depression was also found in about one-fourth of the patients. In the group as a whole, over two-thirds had another concurrent psychiatric disorder (Swedo & Rapoport, 1989). Only 20% of the children and adolescents were judged to have a compulsive personality disorder. Since it occurred in a minority of the cases, compulsive personality disorder cannot be viewed as a necessary condition for developing obsessive-compulsive disorder. However, this rate is far higher than expected in unselected patients. Therefore, a significant association between compulsive personality and the full-blown obsessive-compulsive disorder seems to occur in young patients. But even at a relatively early time in the course of the disorder, it may already be too late to clarify which came first, the compulsive personality or the obsessive-compulsive symptomatology.

Comorbidity of affective and anxiety disorder has been noted also in population studies (Anderson, Williams, McGee, & Silva, 1987; Kashani, McGee, Clarkson, Anderson, Walton, Williams, Silva, Robins, Cytryn, & McKnew, 1983) as well as in nonreferred children of depressed mothers (Weissman, in press). It appears to be a real clinical phenomenon, suggesting common vulnerabilities underlying anxiety and depressive disorders.

However, differences in clinical diagnostic standards make it difficult to compare studies. There are diagnostic confusions in the delineating of depressive disorders in anxiety disorders. For example, school phobic children who miss school or leave school during the day because of somatic complaints (whether due to separation anxiety or social phobias) often avoid contact with their peers. They do so to avoid the embarrassment of having to account for their unusual behavior to their classmates. This change in the children's levels of social activity can be seen as a loss of social interest, and counted as a depressive symptom. Children who are anxious about having to go to school often have difficulties going to sleep due to worrying over the following morning; they may get up during the night, and may be viewed as having insomnia (another depressive symptom). In addition, it is not rare for them to refuse breakfast, and to avoid eating lunch in school — another potential sign of depression. Because they sleep poorly, these children may feel tired and have difficulty concentrating. Moreover, in severe cases demoralization coupled with pessimism can occur, but it is typically circumscribed to school adjustment. All these features are defining clinical criteria of a major depressive disorder. Yet, they can all occur as part of anxious symptomatology. Unless care is taken to clarify the clinical nature of these complaints, it is unlikely that they will be considered to reflect affective dysregulation rather than anxiety. These issues are inadequately specified in the current studies on comorbidity, and greater detail regarding how these symptoms are interpreted will be necessary for the results on comorbidity to be fully understandable.

ANXIETY SYMPTOMS

It is clear that many anxious children have an array of symptoms that justifies one of the childhood or adolescent anxiety disorders. At the same time, we are all familiar with children who have specific fears, such as a fear of doctors, or a fear of school examinations. If the fear is isolated and not part of a more pervasive phobic pattern, the child is considered to have a simple phobia. However, little is known about how often such anxiety symptoms are circumscribed, or how often they reflect a generalized anxiety syndrome. We know of only two studies that have examined this diagnostic question in children.

The correlates of fear of dental treatment were studied in 11 affected children compared to 14 controls (Williams, Murray, Lund, Harkiss, & DeFranco, 1985). Parents rated the fearful children as having had more negative reactions to previous medical treatment but their treatment histories were not worse. They also rated these children as having more mood and social problems. The implications of this small study are that severe fear of medical intervention is likely to be associated with other anxious symptomatology. However, the number of children studied is far too small to venture any general observation.

Test anxiety is another form of specific fear that can render children miserable and incapacitated. Moreover, it can impair performance in an important functional domain. Although a great deal of research has been done on the effect of test anxiety on test performance, remarkably little has appeared on its treatment (only one treatment study has been done [van der Ploeg-Stapert & van der Ploeg, 1986]), or on its clinical significance. Beidel and Turner (1988) have conducted the only clinical study of childhood test anxiety. They compared 25 test anxious children to 25 controls on scale and interview measures. A quarter of the test anxious children received an anxiety disorder diagnosis, while none of the controls did. The two most frequent diagnoses were of social phobia and overanxious disorder. This clinical study also suggests that what appears as a circumscribed specific phobic reaction may be only one symptom of an anxiety disorder that affects multiple aspects of a child's adaptation. Therefore, it is possible that children with specific fears severe enough to impair functioning suffer from one of the anxiety disorders other than simple phobia.

SUMMARY

In this chapter clinical characteristics of the various childhood anxiety disorders were reviewed, and their differential diagnosis and comorbidity were discussed. Although researchers recently have begun to empirically examine the validity (especially, discriminate) of the DSM-III (and DSM-III-R) diagnostic categories (e.g., Last, Hersen, Kazdin, Finkelstein, & Strauss, 1987), considerably more research is needed in this area. Traditional psychiatric methods of validating diagnostic categories — family, follow-up, treatment outcome, and laboratory studies (looking for possible biological markers) — need to be employed as well as more recent innovative statistical (multivariate) approaches. Essentially, the question that remains is whether the DSM-III-Rs nosological system adequately reflects the phenomenology of pathological anxiety in children and adolescents.

3

ASSESSMENT

The assessment of anxiety has a surprisingly long history, emerging as an active endeavor with the advent of sophisticated statistical measures such as factor analysis. This technical advance fostered the development of the first personality tests, several of which initially included an anxiety factor for children. Subsequently, probably because of the central role attributed to anxiety for all types of psychopathology, special scales to quantify anxiety were constructed. Finally, the interest in psychiatric diagnosis fostered by DSM-III stimulated the development of structured diagnostic interviews.

PERSONALITY TESTS

Many of the personality tests developed for children have anxiety items and generate an anxiety factor. Because they were devised as comprehensive assessments for various aspects of personality, they are long. However, in spite of their length they do not include a thorough coverage of the various forms of anxiety.

Probably the most widely used personality tests in the United States are the California Tests of Personality. Four forms are available for different ages from kindergarten through college (Thorpe, Clark, & Tiegs, 1953a; Thorpe, Clark, & Tiegs, 1953b; Clark, Tiegs, & Thorpe, 1953; Tiegs, Clark, & Thorpe, 1953). The anxiety scale includes mostly somatic complaints such as headaches, stomachaches, frequent colds, sneezing spells, eyes hurting, but fails to mention anxious concerns. Since the content is not designed to reflect pathological anxiety, the tests are inappropriate in the clinical setting. In fact, it is not clear whether the California Tests of Personality have any merit for the quantification of anxiety even in the general population.

The Eysenck Personality Questionnaire has a version for children that includes a neuroticism scale that also fails to include worries, fears and anxiety (Eysenck & Eysenck, 1975). Also, it lacks norms, and has no demonstrated validity for the assessment of anxiety.

Cattel, an early pioneer in the assessment of personality, developed several self-rating scales of anxiety for children and adolescents (The Early School Personality Questionnaire, Cattell & Coan 1979; Children's Personality Questionnaire, Porter & Cattell, 1979; High School Personality Questionnaire, Cattell & Cattell, 1979). Scores for many personality traits are provided, several of which appear to reflect children's anxiety level. For example, the scales include assessments that evaluate children as shy versus venturesome, self-assured versus apprehensive, relaxed versus tense. Although the measures provide multiple measures, none is specific and precise in its functional content. As stated by Thorndike (1978), "Cattell has tended to emphasize breadth of coverage at the expense of precision in single scores" (p. 766). Therefore, these personality tests are not satisfactory overall assessments of childhood and adolescent anxiety.

The above personality tests are self-rated measures that require the child to score various fears as they pertain to him or her. A major difficulty is that each child applies different standards to decide whether the fears he or she experiences warrant a positive reply. A particular anxious concern can be judged differently by different children. Some minimize its personal significance, whereas others exaggerate it. As a result, similar ratings reflect quite different levels of subjective anxiety. In addition, the personality tests do not provide an opportunity to rate how the fear or worry affects the child's behavior or well-being. The failure to include behavioral or functional impairment provides another source of confusion in the assessment of anxiety, since children whose ratings are identical may adapt in different fashion to the distress they experience. The stoic ones may expose themselves to phobic situations, while others may avoid them, even if they are only mildly uncomfortable. For these reasons, the utility of personality tests to assess anxiety in children is very limited, and their clinical usefulness is discounted.

Although the paper and pencil personality tests have a history dating back a half century, they were never adopted as standard procedures for the assessment of children in clinical settings. Several historical phenomena are likely explanations for clinicians' lack of interest in these sophisticated instruments. For one, the tests implied an objective quantifiable view of personality that did not conform to the prevailing clinical models of psychopathology, most of them psychoanalytically oriented. Paper and pencil tests were viewed as superficial and trivial to the concerns of clinicians.

In spite of the lack of compatibility between test developers and clinicians, they shared the view that anxiety was a trait, that is, a characteristic intrinsic to the person. The notion that affective states as well as other aspects of behavior were the expression of pervasive personality features subsequently became controversial. Social learning theorists argued that manifest personality was a result of the social interactional context, that emotions reflected responses to specific environmental conditions and were not fixed or stable features of an individual. Therefore, even when behaviorally oriented clinicians became established, personality scales that were based on a trait model of behavior continued to be ignored by clinicians whether they were dynamically or behaviorally oriented.

ANXIETY SCALES

Unlike the personality tests whose item content includes the evaluation of multiple aspects of personality, anxiety scales, as their name indicates, are limited to fears and worries. Some of these scales will be discussed in detail below.

Cattell and his group extracted a 40-item Anxiety Scale, (The IPAT Anxiety Scale) from a broad-based adult personality questionnaire (Cattell, Krug, & Scheier, 1976). It provides norms for high school age, and it has been reported to have demonstrated construct validity (McReynolds, 1978).

State-Trait Anxiety Inventory

The State-Trait Anxiety Inventory (STAI) for Children (Spielberger, 1973) was designed to distinguish between the two types of anxiety its name implies. The child rates him- or herself as he or she feels right now (state), and in general (trait) (the scale does not elicit information about situations that trigger anxiety temporarily). The clinical importance of the child's level of anxiety at the very moment he or she completes the scale is very likely to be trivial at best. It is probably judicious to conceive of this scale as similar to other anxiety scales. It merely provides self-ratings of general levels of anxiety. In a clinical study, the STAI did not differentiate among diagnostic groups of 63 hospitalized patients; however, only 10 of the patients had a diagnosis of anxiety disorder (Hoehn-Saric, Maisami, & Wiegand, 1987). In a study by Strauss and colleagues, the state but not trait measure discriminated between children with pure anxiety disorders and controls (Strauss, Last, Hersen, & Kazdin, 1988).

Children's Manifest Anxiety Scale

In 1956, a child version was published (Castaneda, McCandless, & Palermo, 1956) of the adult Taylor Manifest Anxiety Scale, which had been extracted from the MMPI (Minnesota Multiphasic Personality Inventory) (Hathaway & McKinley, 1951). The Children's Manifest Anxiety Scale consists of 42 anxiety items, and also includes a "lie" scale aimed at providing an index of honesty. The score is simply the sum of items scored *yes*. Subsequently, the scale was rewritten, some items deleted, and others added, to generate 37 items, 25 from the original list, and 9 for a new lie scale (Reynolds & Richmond, 1978; Reynolds & Richmond, 1984). The revised Children's Manifest Anxiety Scale is presented in Table 3.1. The reading level is aimed at the average third grader; therefore, the scale must be administered orally to first and second graders, and to older poor readers. The new scale was refashioned to include statements with internal consistency from ratings provided by several hundred grade school children.

A factor analytic study of the revised Children's Manifest Anxiety Scale reported three factors (Reynolds & Richmond, 1979). Factor 1, which the authors judge reflects physiological signs of anxiety, Factor 2 considered to indicate worry and oversensitivity, and Factor 3 which is labeled Fear/Concentration. The factors generated by the revised scale are very similar to those from a previous factor analysis of the original Children's Manifest Anxiety Scale (Finch, Kendall, & Montgomery, 1974); therefore, it is likely that the scale taps meaningful aspects of children's anxious concerns. A further factor analytic study, conducted in over 4,000 normal youngsters between ages 6 and 19 (very few 18 and 19 year olds were included) suggested that the scale contained three anxiety factors, as previously reported, and two lie factors (See Table 3.2) (Reynolds & Paget, 1981). The authors examined whether differences occurred in factor structure and other scale properties between white and black children, and none were found. In addition to the three specific factors, the factor analysis suggested the presence of a general anxiety factor. The scale may then be used as an overall estimate of anxiety, or as a measure of different forms of anxiety.

TABLE 3.1

Revised Children's Manifest Anxiety Scale and Its Factor Structure

Factor*	Item
1	I have trouble making up my mind.
2	I get nervous when things do not go the right way for me.
3	Others seem to do things easier than I can.
L	I like everyone I know.
1	Often I have trouble getting my breath.
2	I worry a lot of the time.
3	I am afraid of a lot of things.
L	I am always kind.
1	I get mad easily.
2	I worry about what my parents will say to me.
3	I feel that others do not like the way I do things.
L	I always have good manners.
1	It is hard for me to get to sleep at night.
2	I worry about what other people think about me.
3	I feel alone even when there are people with me.
L	I am always good.
1	Often I feel sick in my stomach.
2	My feelings get hurt easily.
3	My hands feel sweaty.
L	I am always nice to everyone.
1	I am tired a lot.
2	I worry about what is going to happen.
3	Other children are happier than I.
L	I tell the truth every single time.
1	I have bad dreams.
2	My feelings get hurt easily when I am fussed at.
3	I feel someone will tell me I do things the wrong way.
L	I never get angry.
1	I wake up scared some of the time.
2	I worry when I go to bed at night.
3	It is hard for me to keep my mind on my schoolwork.
L	I never say things I shouldn't.
1	I wiggle in my seat a lot.
2	I am nervous.
3	A lot of people are against me.
L	I never lie.
2	I often worry about something bad happening to me.

NOTE: Factor 1: Physiological anxiety
Factor 2: Worrying, oversensitivity
Factor 3: Fear/concentration
*L = Lie Scale item

A test-retest reliability study in sixth, seventh, and eighth grade boys and girls indicated good reliability over 1- and 5-week intervals (r's = .88 and .77, respectively) (Wisniewski, Mulick, Genshaft, & Coury, 1987). However, the reliability of two specific factors (Worry-sensitivity and Social-concentration) was mediocre after a 5-week hiatus — only around .60. The adequacy of the very short-term reliability of the Children's Manifest Anxiety Scale in a normal sample is encouraging but does not preclude the necessity for similar reliability from patient data groups since reliability results from one population are not readily generalizable to another. Furthermore, the modest reliabilities over a 1-month period are not encouraging regarding the potential usefulness of the scale for documenting levels of psychopathology or treatment response in children with anxiety disorders.

Support for the construct validity of the scale was obtained by Reynolds (1980) who found it to correlate highly with trait anxiety on the State-Trait Anxiety for Children. In contrast, the revised manifest anxiety scale scores and ratings of state anxiety did not correlate. Similar results were found in a small group of hospitalized children with anxiety disorders (Hoehn-Saric, Maisami, & Wiegand, 1987). To its credit, the revised manifest anxiety scale seems to reflect relatively stable feelings rather than those that occur while children are completing the scale. However, several words of caution are in order.

In the correlational study by Reynolds (1980), children who had been referred to a clinic were utilized, yet their scores were not deviant. The low anxiety scores were all the more surprising since almost a third of the children were described as presenting with emotional disorders, and one would expect such children to be more anxious than normals, especially at the time they are referred for professional attention. Others have not found it to distinguish clinical groups, although the samples studied have been very small (Hoehn-Saric, Maisami, & Wiegand, 1987). Therefore, one must be cautious in drawing clinical conclusions from scores obtained on the Children's Manifest Anxiety Scale. In a clinic study of children with DSM-III diagnoses, one factor of the Children's Manifest Anxiety Scale (Worry/Oversensitivity) significantly distinguished between the anxiety disorders and other psychiatric diagnoses; in addition, significantly more of the children with anxiety disorders had elevated scores on this factor (40% vs. 19%) (Mattison, Bagnato, & Brubaker, 1988). The other two factor scores did not differentiate the clinical groups. These differences, though significant do not document the validity of the scale for the clinical purpose

TABLE 3.2

Five-Factor Solution for the Total National Normative Sample (N = 4,972) of the Revised Children's Manifest Anxiety Scale

Item	Anxiety Factor			Lie Factor	
	1 Physiological	2 Worry/ oversensitivity	3 Concentration	1	2
1. I have trouble making up my mind.	x				
2. I get nervous when things do not go the right way for me.		x			
3. Others seem to do things easier than I can.			x		
4. I like everyone I know.				x	
5. Often I have trouble getting my breath.	x				
6. I worry a lot of the time.		x			
7. I am afraid of a lot of things.		x			
8. I am always kind.				x	
9. I get mad easily.	x				
10. I worry about what my parents will say to me.		x			
11. I feel that others do not like the way I do things.			x		
12. I always have good manners.				x	
13. It is hard for me to get to sleep at night.	x				
14. I worry about what other people think about me.		x			
15. I feel alone even when there are people with me.			x		
16. I am always good.				x	
17. Often I feel sick in my stomach.	x				
18. My feelings get hurt easily.		x			
19. My hands feel sweaty.	x				

Item					
20. I am always nice to everyone.				x	
21. I am tired a lot.	x				
22. I worry about what is going to happen.		x			
23. Other children are happier than I.		x			
24. I tell the truth every single time.				x	
25. I have bad dreams.	x				
26. My feelings get hurt easily when I am fussed at.		x			
27. I feel someone will tell me I do things the wrong way.			x		
28. I never get angry.					x
29. I wake up scared some of the time.	x				
30. I worry when I go to bed at night.		x			
31. It is hard for me to keep my mind on my schoolwork.			x		
32. I never say things I shouldn't.					x
33. I wiggle in my seat a lot.	x				
34. I am nervous.		x			
35. A lot of people are against me.			x		
36. I never lie.					x
37. I often worry about something bad happening to me.		x			
Eigenvalue	2.24	2.84	1.59	2.95	.98
% Variance	34	42	24	75	25

NOTES: x Factor on which item has the highest loading (.23 to .61 for factors 1, 2, 3).

of identifying children with anxiety disorders. Of such cases, 60% will be missed by the scale. Of the children without anxiety disorders, 20% will be misidentified as anxious. Furthermore, a group of purely anxious clinic children did not rate themselves as more anxious than controls in the study by Strauss, Last, Hersen, and Kazdin (1988).

The hope of accurate classification by means of self-rating anxiety scale is probably unrealistic. This limitation certainly diminishes the usefulness of the scale, but does not eliminate it. If reliable, it can still offer meaningful information concerning quantitative aspects of anxiety in children whose diagnoses have been established through proper clinical evaluations. Finally, the notion that the lie factor identifies bias, as it is claimed to do, has been questioned and pointedly critiqued (Sarason, 1966). The fact that the lie factor has been found to have rather poor reliability (Wisniewski et al., 1987) raises further questions about its usefulness.

Fear Survey for Children

To evaluate children's fears in a number of contexts, Scherer & Nakamura (1968) devised an 80-item scale for children ages 9 through 12—the Fear Survey Schedule for Children, modeled after a similar questionnaire used with adults (The Wolpe-Lang Fear Survey, Wolpe & Lang, 1964). Several factors have been generated, but from a sample too small to permit the confident use of the factor structure. Ollendick (1983) used the fear survey to contrast school phobic and normal children. Encouragingly, he found that school phobic children referred for treatment obtained significantly higher scores than controls, though considerable overlap between the two groups occurred. This overlap precludes using the scale scores to classify children as anxious versus nonanxious. However, as Ollendick notes, the survey could be used to identify children with relatively elevated scores in casefinding procedures, in which one is interested in targeting children for further study. Very adequate score consistency was obtained over a brief 1-week interval (r = .82). Not surprisingly, the test-retest reliability was less satisfactory after a 3-month hiatus (r = .55). The scores on the Fear Survey schedule correlated only moderately with the trait measure of The State-Trait Anxiety Inventory (r's = .46 and .51). Therefore, though the two scales weakly tap some common characteristic, they cannot be viewed as measures that assess the same psychological phenomenon. This finding is different from the reported very high relationship between the Manifest Anxiety Scale and the trait anxiety measure of the State-Trait Anxiety Inventory (Reynolds, 1980).

In the study by Strauss, Last, Hersen, and Kazdin (1988), the Fear Survey (as well as the Trait Anxiety Scale of the STAIC and the Children's Manifest Anxiety Scale) failed to discriminate between anxiety disordered children and controls. Only one study has used the Fear Survey to contrast children who had received DSM-III diagnoses of anxiety disorders (Last, Francis, & Strauss, in press). In the diagnostic groups studied, separation anxiety and overanxious disorders did not differ in overall level of self-rated fear. This finding is not unexpected since both groups had an anxiety disorder severe enough to warrant clinical attention. However, more problematically, the two diagnostic groups did not differ on any of the five factor scores (fear of failure and criticism, fear of the unknown, fear of injury and small animals, fear of danger and death, and medical fears). The diagnostic characteristics of each disorder would lead to the expectation that overanxious children should have higher levels of fear of criticism and medical fears, whereas separation anxious youngsters should have relatively elevated levels of fear of danger and death. As currently designed, the scale does not seem to provide diagnostically relevant distinctions, but it may be useful as a means of quantifying levels of anxiety without regard to subtypes of anxiety.

Comment

If the self-rating anxiety scales are tapping a meaningful common psychological construct, they should have relatively good consistency. The intercorrelational values obtained have varied, but on the whole fairly good agreement has been obtained on various measures. Only one study has examined the three main instruments in the same cohort (Strauss, Lease, Last, & Francis, 1988). In a group of 40 children with overanxious disorder, the authors found strikingly good associations between the total score of the Children's Manifest Anxiety Scale and the Fear Survey Schedule ($r = .79$) and both the state and trait measures of the State-Trait Anxiety Inventory (r's $= .70$ and $.79$). The associations between the Fear Survey and the State-Trait inventory were only modest, however (r's $= .41$ and $.52$). The study also obtained self-ratings on a commonly used depression scale (the Children's Depression Inventory [Kovacs, 1983a]). This measure, which is purported to reflect a different component of children's psychological state, correlated as well with the anxiety scale scores as the latter did among themselves. Furthermore, in the Strauss et al. study (1988), the anxious children with a concurrent depressive disorder rated themselves as more anxious than controls, whereas those with pure anxiety did not. The mixed depressed/anxious children also had higher levels of scale ratings of anxiety than did the purely anxious children. Such a lack of discrimination in affective assessment makes one wonder what is being measured with anxiety self-rating scales.

All the above anxiety scales for children are self-rating scales. Therefore, they incur the same concerns as the paper and pencil personality tests mentioned previously. There are no standards provided for evaluating the severity of a fear or worry, and individuals vary in threshold for reporting distress; in addition, the degree of functional impairment is not detectable. The Children's Manifest Anxiety Scale and the State-Trait Anxiety Inventory for Children have a 2-point scoring, requiring a *yes* or *no* choice. In contrast, the Fear Survey Schedule for Children provides gradations of scoring that make it far more useful for detecting change over time or with treatment. The only available scale specifically designed for the assessment of obsessive-compulsive symptoms, the Leyton Obsessional Inventory — Child Version, is an exception (Berg, Rapoport, & Flament, 1985). The inventory provides a "resistance" rating that provides the opportunity for children (ages 8 to 18) to indicate the degree to which the obsessive-compulsive symptomatology affects their daily living. The measure has demonstrated reliability and has been found to reflect clinical improvement in controlled treatment studies (Flament, Rapoport, Berg, Sceery, Kilts, Mellstrom, & Linnoila, 1985; Leonard, Swedo, Rapoport, Coffey, & Cheslow, 1988). However, like the other self-rating instruments, it is not a diagnostic instrument.

It may not be possible to construct a self-rated instrument that can reflect reliably important but complicated distinctions in the various forms of anxiety. It most likely requires a clinically trained evaluator to differentiate phenomenological variations in anxiety. Indeed, this conclusion was supported in a clinical examination of hospitalized children who received clinical interview assessments of anxiety, and two self-rating anxiety scales, the State-Trait Anxiety Inventory and the revised Children's Manifest Anxiety Scale (Hoehn-Saric, Maisami, & Wiegand, 1987).

PARENT SCALES

For the purpose of obtaining a large amount of information about children's adjustment in a rapid and economical fashion, parent- and teacher-rated behavior scales have been devised. As is the case for the personality tests, they aim to sample a broad spectrum of psychopathology; consequently, they cannot provide detailed coverage for each type of dysfunction. All the scales have been factor analyzed, and some provide an anxiety scale.

One of the oldest parent rating scales, the Louisville Behavior Checklist, (Miller, 1967a, 1967b), includes an 11-item anxiety factor (the items are listed in Table 3.3). The factor analysis was conducted on parental ratings *(yes/no)* of boys, 6 to 12 years of age, coming to a clinic for treatment. The anxiety factor represents the types of parent-perceived behaviors that cluster together in a male patient group, but it cannot be viewed as reflecting the way the items would sort themselves in a normal population. Therefore, it could be used to evaluate how anxious a child is rated compared to unselected patients, but not compared to normals. As can be seen from the item content, the multiforms of anxiety are poorly reflected in the anxiety factor. Furthermore, several items that clearly reflect anxiety (for example, phobic, afraid at night, fearful), appear on factors other than the anxiety factor.

The anxiety scale was revised to provide better internal consistency and better face validity. The modified scale reflects relevant clinical aspects of childhood anxiety and is much more satisfactory than its predecessor (Miller, Barrett, Hampe, & Noble, 1971). This effort is a good example of how a statistically derived anxiety factor is irrelevant to clinical reality, and how further improvements are possible. The renamed Fear Scale included in Table 3.3 taps specific fears (trains, loud noises), as well as general anxiety and separation anxiety.

The scores obtained for boys and girls (500 school children, grades 2 through 7) were very similar (Miller, Hampe, Barrett, & Noble, 1971). A child whose parent endorsed 12 or more scale items would fall in the top percentile of the general population. On average, the normal children received positive scores on somewhat fewer than two items, about 50% were rated positive on three anxiety statements.

The same investigators developed a parent-rated fear questionnaire for children. The Louisville Fear Survey is a list of 60 fears, administered to parents or children (ages 4 through 18). The list was derived from clinical judgments and culled from other fear inventories (Miller, Barrett, Hampe, & Noble, 1972). The parent ratings of normal children

TABLE 3.3

Item Content of Anxiety Factors on Major Behavior Rating Scales

Scale: Louisville Behavior Check List
Raters: Parents
Scoring: Yes/No
Items: Headaches; migraine headaches; stomach-ache-somatic; fear of school; worries—
guilty; complains not loved easily; feels pain more; says "picked on"; feels inferior; cries

Scale: Louisville Behavior Check List Fear Scale
Raters: Parents
Scoring: Yes/No
Items: Dependent on others; unable to do things for himself or herself; tosses and turns in sleep, rolls, gets up often at night, etc. (poor or restless sleeping); demands special attention or fusses at bedtime; says he or she is not as good as others; feels inferior; afraid of such things as the dark, thunderstorms, domestic animals; wants or demands that someone sleep with him or her; always worrying that he or she or someone else is going to die; fearful, constantly afraid; worries all the time or feels very guilty; worries that parents may get hurt or sick or die; at times afraid he or she is going to die; is afraid that he or she will see or hear something frightening at night; complains of bad drams or nightmares; very much afraid of loud noises; afraid of being in cars, trains, airplanes, or elevators; takes things in stride, not easily upset; becomes "jittery"; builds up tension, becomes "wound up"; worries about disasters such as hurricanes, wars, fires at school, air raids

Scale: Personality Inventory for Children (PIC)
Rater: Parent
Scoring: Yes/No
Items (Positive): My child worries about things that usually only adults worry about; my child is worried about sin; my child has little self-confidence; thunder and lightning bother my child; my child often asks if I love him or her; my child seems too serious minded; often my child is afraid of little things; my child worries about talking to others; my child frequently has nightmares; my child seems fearful of blood; my child is easily embarrassed; my child will worry a lot before starting something new; my child often has crying spells; my child broods some; my child is afraid of dying; my child seems unhappy about our home life; others often remark how moody my child is; my child insists on keeping the light on while sleeping; my child is afraid of the dark
Items (Negative): My child is as happy as ever; my child is usually in good spirits; my child usually looks at the bright side of things; usually my child takes things in stride; my child takes criticism easily; nothing seems to scare my child

(continued)

and of a clinical group of phobic children were subjected to factor analysis. Three factors emerged: *Factor I* includes items related to separation, such as threats to the well-being of the family or to the child; *Factor II* reflects fear of natural events, such as lightning, thunder, and so on, and *Factor III* mostly concerns anxiety about performance and

TABLE 3.3 Continued

Scale: Child Behavior Checklist
Rater: Parent
Scoring: Not true, somewhat or sometimes true, very true, or often true
Items: Girls 4 - 5
Obsessions; clings to adults; cries much; demands attention; fears; feels persecuted; hears things; nervous; anxious; sees thing; sleeps little; strange behavior; can't sleep; whining
Boys 4 - 5
none
Girls 6 - 11
none
Boys 6 - 11
Clings to adults; fears; fears school; hears things that aren't there; overconforms; anxious; sleeps in class; sees things that aren't there; shy, timid
Girls 12-16
Obsession; lonely; cries much; jealous; fears; fears school; fears own impulses; needs to be perfect; feels unloved; feels persecuted; feels worthless; nervous; nightmares; anxious; feels guilty; self-conscious; sleeps little; can't sleep; worrying
Boys 12 - 16
none

Scale: Child Behavior Checklist
Raters: Teachers
Scoring: Not true, somewhat or sometimes true, very true, or often true
Items: Girls 6 - 11
Clings to adults*; fears; fears own impulses*; needs to be perfect *; feels worthless*; nervous; overconforms*; anxious*; feels guilty*; self-conscious*; shy; timid*; feels hurt when criticized*; too neat*; sad; anxious to please*; fears mistakes*; worrying*
Boys 6 - 11
Starred items (*) of anxiety factor in girls 6-11, plus secretive
Girls 12 - 16
Clings to adults^x; cries; fears^x; fears own impulses^x; needs to be perfect^x; feels worthless^x; nail biting^x; nervous^x; overconforms^x; anxious^x; feels guilty^x; self-conscious^x; shy, timid^x; feels hurt when criticized^x anxious to please^x; fears mistakes^x; whining; worrying^x
Boys 12 - 16
Crossed items (^{x}) of anxiety factor for Girls 12 - 16, plus lonely; jealous; feels unloved; feels persecuted; easily frustrated; too neat; sad

social ridicule. None of these is pure with regard to the type of anxiety it reflects. It should not be assumed on the basis of factor analysis that factors represent discrete, mutually exclusive clinical characteristics. It is very likely that fearful children obtain high scores on all three, or two of the three factors, rather than only one of the three. It would be erroneous to conclude from the factor analysis, that the Louisville Fear

Survey has identified separate syndromes of anxiety. However, it could be a helpful measure to identify specific sources of difficulty. It is quite similar to the Fear Survey Schedule but has the marked advantage of being applicable to a wider age group. For unknown reasons, this scale never became popular and has not been used widely. Perhaps it is that is never provided for a teacher-rated version. It is generally believed that teachers provide more reliable and valued information about children's behavior than parents do, since teachers are able to judge children with a built-in standard for what is average behavior for the child's age and sex. Yet, when assessing affective states such as anxiety and depression, parents are felt to be critical sources of information and teachers may not offer an advantage over evaluations derived from other informants. However, this point requires empirical confirmation.

Taking inspiration from the well-established MMPI, a group of investigators developed a similar instrument to be completed by parents about their children. The Personality Inventory for Children, known as the PIC, includes 600 items rated true or false. The whole questionnaire or selected sub-scales can be used so the rating scale can be tailored to meet particular needs or interests. The factors were not only derived from statistical investigation, but also from clinicians' judgments. The content of the anxiety factor is presented in Table 3.3. It has good internal reliability, and good short-term test-retest consistency. Extensive work has been done with the scale and it provides general population norms for children of preschool age through adolescence (Lachar, 1982; Wirt, Lachar, Klinedinst, & Seat, 1977). More recently, the scale has been used with teachers. Examining the offspring of adult patients with anxiety or depressive disorders, Sylvester, Hyde, and Reichler (1987) found significant but very modest relationships between DSM-III anxiety disorders obtained from structured clinical interviews with parent and child and pathological scores on the anxiety scales of the PIC. Although considerable evidence has been accumulated concerning the validity of many aspects of the scale, it has not been studied in relationship to clinical cases of anxiety disorders in children and its usefulness in this specific area is in question.

Some of the most widely used rating scales are the Conners Parent and Conners Teacher Rating Scales (Goyette, Conners, & Ulrich, 1978). These have been shown to be extremely helpful for the assessment of hyperactive children and for tracking their treatment response. The parent but not the teacher scale provides an anxiety factor. The scale has not been used in groups where its usefulness for the detection of anxiety and its reduction with treatment can be assessed. However, it probably should not. It has a very limited sampling of anxiety, and is not suitable for the assessment of childhood anxiety.

Achenbach and colleagues have carried out a major effort to provide norms for parent- and teacher-rated behavior of children, boys and girls, between ages 6 through 16 (The Child Behavior Checklist, Achenbach, 1978; Achenbach & Edelbrock, 1979). Like the PIC, the Child Behavior Checklist (CBC) provides very well established norms for each sex at each age, enabling a relatively confident judgment as to the degree of deviance. However, the checklist has real limitations of the assessment of anxiety. An anxiety factor was obtained for girls ages 4 to 5 and 12 to 16, but not for 6 to 11 year olds. Yet, there is no reason to believe that anxiety is a less relevant aspect of function in 6- to 11-year-old girls than other ages.

For boys, the picture is equally puzzling: An anxiety factor was derived in 6 to 11 year olds only (the age group in which no anxiety factor was obtained in girls), but not for the 4- to 5- and 12- to 16-year-old boys. Complicating features in the application of the scales include the divergent content of the anxiety factors for boys and girls of the same ages and for each gender at different ages. The differences are readily observable from a perusal of the item content of the anxiety scores presented in Table 3.3. The age and sex differences raise question concerning the construct validity of the anxiety factors (i.e., what do they really measure?), since it is generally observed that there are no qualitative differences between boys and girls in the nature of the anxieties they experience. From many surveys, the nature of fears and anxiety does not appear to differ between boys and girls (though their magnitude sometimes does). The age and sex asymmetry of the CBC anxiety factor as well as the lack of inconsistency in the items that make up the anxiety factors (when they are derived) preclude comparisons between boys and girls and across age groups within and between genders. Therefore, the checklist has limited usefulness for the assessment of anxiety in children. In a small study comparing overanxious, dysthymic, and hyperactive children, the number of children with standard scores in the pathological range did not differentiate the three diagnostic groups (Mattison & Bagnato, 1987).

As is the case for other rating scales, the Child Behavior Checklist does not allow important decisions and clinical judgments to be reached about specific children. The PIC and the Child Behavior Profile are probably best seen as ways of identifying major areas of difficulty and as signals to look further through clinical assessment. Both these instruments have the shortcoming of requiring two- or three-point decisions for item ratings. For clinical purposes, this is a disadvantage since it limits the possibility of subtle rankings and of detecting change. However, the scales have many other virtues, such as acceptability by parents and teachers, well-established reliability, and some evidence of validity (but not for anxiety specifically). They represent a major advance in the assessment of childhood psychopathology, if not anxiety.

STRUCTURED DIAGNOSTIC INTERVIEWS

All the clinical systematic interviews include a version for interviewing the child and another for use with the parent. Though it has been argued that the interview with the child provides no information above and beyond what is obtained from the parent (Rutter, 1976), this observation cannot be assumed to be true for all types of psychopathology. For the assessment of anxiety, which represents an internal state, the child's report may provide information that the parent's does not. Furthermore, the degree to which parents' and children's reports overlap depends not only on the type of information asked about, but also the age of the child. At all ages, a proper evaluation demands that information be inquired from multiple sources.

The first clinical interview (Graham & Rutter, 1968; Rutter & Graham, 1968) provides a single overall category for anxiety disorders. The more recent interviews appeared after the DSM-III classification and therefore provide diagnoses for the anxiety disorders included in the diagnostic manual. There are four elaborately structured interviews in use with children — all include an assessment of anxiety: Diagnostic Interview Schedule for Children (DIS-C) (Costello, Edelbrock, Kessler, Kalas, & Klaric, 1983); Diagnostic Interview for Children and Adolescents (DICA) (Reich, Herjanic, Welner, & Gandhy, 1982), and Schedule for Affective Disorders and Schizophrenia for School-Age Children (Kiddie-SADS or K-SADS) (Chambers, Puig-Antich, Hirsch, Paez, Ambrosini, Tabrizi, & Davies, 1985); and Interview Schedule for Children (ISC) (Kovacs, 1983b). If they are administered in their entirety, they are very time consuming. However, for purposes of assessing the presence of anxiety disorders, one could select the specifically relevant sections. The K-SADS and the ISC contain extensive inquiry about anxiety symptoms and provide comprehensive coverage for the DSM-III-R anxiety disorders of childhood. To illustrate the approaches used in these assessments, Table 3.4 presents the section on separation anxiety from the K-SADS.

Several investigators have examined the reliability of the clinical interviews of children in the general population and in patient groups (Hoehn-Saric, Maisami, & Wiegand, 1987; Last, 1987; Last, Hersen, Kazdin, Finkelstein, & Strauss, 1987; Strober, Green, & Carlson, 1981). The reliabilities for anxiety disorders are extremely variable. It seems that when used in clinics for children with anxiety disorders by expert interviewers, reliability is good, otherwise it is mediocre, if not worse. It would seem, therefore, that the assessment of anxiety disorders requires clinical refinement sources of unreliability identified. Nevertheless, these interviews are extremely helpful in guiding the manner in which one can approach children to assess the presence of an anxiety disorder. A semistructured interview specifically designed to assess anxiety disorders in 6 to 18 year olds, the ADIS (Anxiety Disorders Interview Schedule for Children), has a version for the child and parent (Silverman & Nelles, 1988). A group of children, 21 from clinic referrals and 30 from the offspring of adult patients with anxiety disorders, and their parents were interviewed. Moderate interrater agreement was obtained for the anxiety disorders from interviews with children and parents. Much better reliability was obtained on symptom subscale scores than the diagnostic assignments. A recent study of a revised version of the Diagnostic Interview Schedule for Children (DISC-R) in a clinical population reported excellent reliability for the diagnoses of separation anxiety disorder from parent and child interviews (Shaffer, Schonfeld, O'Connor, Stokman, Trautman, Shafer, & Ng, 1988).

PSYCHOLOGICAL TESTS

Structured psychological tests, such as the individual intelligence tests, and the unstructured or otherwise known as projective tests have been used to infer the presence of pathological level of anxiety in children. Other measures as well that were not designed to assess personality constructs, such as the BenderGestalt and the Draw-A-Person tests, have been used for similar purposes. All the work done with these measures occurred before the current standards for diagnosing anxiety disorders. Therefore, it is completely obscure to what extent the inferences made about anxiety as derived from these test results reflect the presence of anxiety disorders. In the adult literature it has often been claimed that relatively low scores on the arithmetic and

TABLE 3.4
K-SADS Interview with Child for Separation Anxiety Disorder

Refers to feeling of anxiety ("butterflies in the stomach," nervousness, scary feelings) in connection with separation from mother or other important attachment figures. A series of symptoms frequently accompanies separation anxiety and they are listed below. Such accompanying symptoms point to the presence of separation anxiety and help to assess its severity but they should not substitute for the report from the child or the mother of anxiety on separation from his or her family or home. Refusal to go to school should not be taken as proof of separation anxiety unless there is other concomitant evidence of it, especially feelings of anxiety on separation. Rater should begin by inquiring about the manifestations listed below and later ask for separation anxiety proper, and rate severity.

0   No information.

1   Not at all: Appears indifferent to separations.

2   Slight: Occasionally feels somewhat anxious but not clinically significant.

3   Mild: Often feels anxious about usual separations from parents. Afraid to go to school but no school absences, and no social impairment outside the home.

4   Moderate: Quite anxious. occasional school refusal where he or she stays home or with the parent clinging to parent or out-of-home social impairment (can't go to sleep over friend's house).

5   Severe: Separation anxiety intense and/or has more than $\frac{1}{3}$ of school days over a 1 month period during present episode or at least 3 days in last week and/or regularly has 4 or 5 of the manifestations listed below either out-of-home social impairment (i.e., goes to school under duress but unable to work there because of his or her anxiety).

6   Extreme: Intense separation anxiety and/or has been absent for more than $\frac{2}{3}$ of school days over a 1 month period during present episode or the whole of last week, and/or panic attacks in the context of separation experiences

WHAT ABOUT DURING THE LAST WEEK?   LAST WEEK: 0 1 2 3 4 5 6

TABLE 3.4 Continued

School Refusal/Reluctance	0 No information / NA
	1 No
(Differentiate from truancy.) Needs strong re-	2 Doubtful
peated parental pressure to attend school.	3 Mild to moderate
	4 Severe

Have you been going to school?
How many times have you been absent since
   (onset of episode)?
What happens when you have to go to school?
Do you have any worries about being in school?
What are they?
Do you get any scary feelings about going to
   school?
Tell me about these feelings?
What are you afraid of? Have you ever left
   school?
Where do you go when you leave school?
Do you go home or do you go somewhere else?

	LAST WEEK:	0 1 2 3 4

*Nausea, vomiting, stomachaches, headaches,
only on school days or separation days.*

Do you ever get sick in your stomach or throw	CURRENT EPISODE:	0 1 2 3 4
up or get stomachaches?		
When? In the morning, at night, at school?		
What about during weekends?	LAST WEEK:	0 1 2 3 4

Fear of sleeping away at friend's home.

These scary feelings that you get when you go to	CURRENT EPISODE:	0 1 2 3 4
school, do you get these same feelings if you		
have to sleep away from home?		
Have you slept away from home since (onset of		
episode)		
Why not?	LAST WEEK:	0 1 2 3 4

Fear of sleeping alone.

Do you sleep alone or with your parents?	CURRENT EPISODE:	0 1 2 3 4
Are you afraid of sleeping alone?		
Since when have you been sleeping with your		
parents?	LAST WEEK:	0 1 2 3 4

(continued)

TABLE 3.4 Continued

Preoccupation with thoughts of harm befalling parents or himself or herself when separated.

Do you ever worry about something bad happening to your parents? Like what?	CURRENT EPISODE:	0 1 2 3 4
Are you afraid that they will leave you and not come back?		
Were you afraid of this before (onset of episode)?		
When you are not with your parents are you afraid something bad might happen to you?		
Like what?	LAST WEEK:	0 1 2 3 4

Difficulty falling asleep.

Do you fall asleep right away when you go to bed?	CURRENT EPISODE: LAST WEEK:	0 1 2 3 4

Nightmares with manifest content similar to daytime preoccupations.

What do you think about?	CURRENT EPISODE:	0 1 2 3 4
Do you get nightmares?		
Tell me about them.	LAST WEEK:	0 1 2 3 4

Clinging, demanding behavior with parents (or shadowing).

When you are home do you follow your mother wherever she goes?	CURRENT EPISODE:	0 1 2 3 4
Do you get upset if she is not in the same room with you?	LAST WEEK:	0 1 2 3 4

Fear of being alone in the house.

How do you feel when your parents go out without you?	CURRENT EPISODE:	0 1 2 3 4
Are you afraid to be alone in the house?	LAST WEEK:	0 1 2 3 4

Temper tantrums when separated or when anticipation separations.

Do you get mad when your mother is going out without you?	CURRENT EPISODE:	0 1 2 3 4
Or when you have to go to school?		
What do you do?	LAST WEEK:	0 1 2 3 4

TABLE 3.4 Continued

Fear of getting lost.

| Are you afraid of getting lost when you go out with your mother or father? | CURRENT EPISODE: | 0 1 2 3 4 |
| | LAST WEEK: | 0 1 2 3 4 |

Repeated instances of social withdrawal or apathy or difficulty concentrating when away from parent.

| Do you have trouble playing with friends or paying attention when your parent is not there? | CURRENT EPISODE: | 0 1 2 3 4 |
| | LAST WEEK: | 0 1 2 3 4 |

Parent has to be present during interview.

Are you afraid that she or he will leave while you and I are talking?

0 N/A
1 No
2 Yes

If patient was also diagnosed as major depression or dysthymia, indicate the chronological order of the two conditions.

0 No information, not clear, or N/A
1 Separation anxiety started first.
2 Simultaneous onset.
3 Depression started first.

coding subtests of the Wechsler Intelligence scales reflect anxiety. These same tests are used not only to infer impaired attention such as is present in children with Attention Deficit Disorder with Hyperactivity but also the presence of interfering anxiety. The Wechsler Intelligence Scale for Children has had such a poor record for purposes of clinical diagnosis that it would be most surprising if it offered any help in the assessment of anxiety disorders. As noted in previous reviews (Gittelman, 1980; Gittelman-Klein, 1978) the tests have been shown to distinguish children referred to psychiatric clinics from normals. However, there is no evidence that the tests are useful in discriminating among different types of psychopathology. Sadly, it must be concluded that the psychological tests available to-date do not offer a useful resource for the psychodiagnosis of children. Whether they can be applied to generate more subtle inferences about children's psychological adjustment is not clear. Anxiety has not been examined. The only personality traits that have been studied are aggression, self-esteem, and concern about loss (Gittelman, 1980).

OTHER ASSESSMENTS

Because the behavioral therapeutic approaches require detailed assessment of function before treatment, many techniques have been developed to observe children's fearful behavior by behaviorally oriented therapists and researchers. However, these procedures are complicated, and are best undertaken by experts; they are cumbersome and mostly relevant to assessment for research purposes. Those interested in this specialized area of assessment may refer to a comprehensive review by Barrios, Hartmann, & Shigetomi (1981). It has been suggested that some speech characteristics may be valid indicators of anxiety (Kotsopoulos & Mellor, 1986), notably breath rate, which may be increased in anxious children, and output of speech per breath, which may be decreased.

SUMMARY

There are several approaches to the systematic assessment of anxiety in children, but within each there are limited options. None of the assessments or instruments reviewed provides a complete or adequate evaluation of childhood anxiety disorders. This restriction does not preclude their use. Many of the measures discussed can be applied to obtain a global though limited picture of children's anxiety levels. These must be followed by a fuller clinical assessment for proper evaluation. The overriding merit of the self-rating scales and other behavior-rating scales is that they are cheap, rapid, and convenient. The best strategy is to view currently available scales as means to signal the possible presence of pathological levels of anxiety with the expectation that further investigation is required. The current diagnostic interview schedules provide a consistent means for assessing symptomatology, but their validity in the identification of anxiety disorders is defined in DSM-III has not been assessed fully.

4

TREATMENT

In this chapter we summarize the major strategies reported in the treatment of childhood and adolescent anxiety disorders. There is a sizable clinical literature on behavioral and pharmacological interventions. Psychotherapies other than behavior therapies are used widely to treat anxiety disorders, but there is no body of clinical or empirical information concerning their usefulness. The lack of coverage in psychotherapy in the chapter is a reflection of this lack.

BEHAVIORAL TREATMENTS

Behavioral treatment approaches to childhood anxiety disorders for the most part have been derived from the adult treatment literature, adapted accordingly for use with children and adolescents. The application of these procedures in the treatment of separation anxiety disorder, overanxious disorder, avoidant disorder, and obsessive-compulsive disorder is summarized below.

Separation Anxiety Disorder and "School Phobia"

Over the past 20 years, numerous case reports and single-case studies have described the application of behavioral techniques to the treatment of separation anxious and school phobic children and adolescents. Reports on youngsters exhibiting anxiety-based school refusal have shown successful utilization of several behavioral procedures: graduated in vivo exposure ("in vivo desensitization") (e.g., Ayllon, Smith, & Rogers, 1970; Montenegro, 1968; Patterson, 1965; Perkin, Rowe, & Farmer, 1973; Phillips & Wolpe, 1981), contingency management (e.g., Hersen, 1970; Vaal, 1973; Welch & Carpenter, 1970), flooding (e.g., Smith & Sharpe, 1970), and cognitive-behavioral therapy (Mansdorf & Lukens, 1987).

In addition to the above, several multiple-case series have been published over the years. Kennedy (1965) reported successful treatment of 50 cases of Type I (first episode, acute cases) school phobics treated with in vivo flooding. Smith (1970) reported good outcome for 45 of 49 school phobics treated with either outpatient therapy, inpatient hospitalization, or change of school. The relative efficacy of the three treatments were not reported. In a report by Baker and Wills (1978), 99 school phobics were divided into acute and chronic categories according to Berg's criteria (i.e., acute case defined as at least three years problem-free prior to the present episode of illness). In reviewing the types of treatments provided to these youngsters, results clearly indicated that the vast majority (95%) of acute school phobics were treated with psychotherapy, often in conjunction with tranquilizers (46%) and/or part-time school (33%). By contrast, the majority (69%) of chronic school phobics were treated with "pressure" (most probably in vivo flooding), often administered in conjunction with psychotherapy (67%) and/or tranquilizers (33%). It is interesting to note that not one of the chronic school refusers were offered part-time school, and that only 2% of the acute school refusers were "pressured." Baker and Wills (1978) reported that 89% of both the acute and chronic groups showed a return to school. Moreover, a very favorable outcome (i.e., "symptoms completely gone and no others have occurred") was achieved in 67% of the acute group and 75% of the chronic group.

To the authors' knowledge, only two comparative studies have appeared to date in the literature (Blagg & Yule, 1984; Miller, Barrett, Hampe, & Noble, 1972), and only the Miller et al. study was properly controlled in that the investigators used random assignment. Miller, Barrett, Hampe, and Noble (1972) investigated the treatment of childhood phobias by comparing the efficacy of systematic desensitization, psychotherapy, and a waiting list control group. Although the authors included children with a variety of types of phobias in their sample, the majority (69%) were said to present with school phobia. Outcome measures included parent and nontreating clinician ratings of improvement, and parent behavior checklists that focused on childhood fears. Parental reports of improvement indicated that both active treatments were more effective than the waiting list control condition, with no significant difference between the two active treatment conditions. By contrast, clinician ratings of improvement showed no difference between the three conditions. Unfortunately, results are not reported separately for the school phobic subgroup.

In a naturalistic study, Blagg and Yule (1984) compared the effectiveness of three treatment conditions: in vivo flooding (n = 30), inpatient hospitalization (n = 16), and home tutoring plus psychotherapy (n = 20) for a group of children identified as school phobic using Berg's criteria. Children were categorized according to Kennedy's criteria as Type I or Type II school refusers. The authors report that half the children in the behavioral treatment group, three-quarters of the children in the hospitalized group, and one-quarter of the children in the home tutoring group were classified as Type II (i.e., more seriously disturbed, chronic cases). These differences were not statistically significant.

The behavioral treatment consisted of frequent contact with school personnel, strategies for use by the parents (e.g., praising school attendance while ignoring physical complaints), and in vivo flooding, using procedures similar to those reported by Kennedy (1965). The inpatient hospitalization treatment consisted of the physical separation of the parent and child, therapeutic milieu, attendance at the inpatient school, possible medication intervention, and discharge school placement planning. Finally, in the home-tutoring condition the child was permitted to remain at home while receiving educational tutoring and psychotherapy.

Outcome measures included several measures of overall emotional adjustment and a record of school attendance. Results indicated that 93% of children in the behavioral treatment condition attended school without problems or with minor, easily remedied problems at the end of the treatment trial. This was in marked contrast to the success rates for inpatient hospitalization (37%) and home tutoring (10%). In addition, children in the behavioral treatment condition showed improvement on measures of self-esteem and extroversion. Finally, children in the behavioral treatment group received an average of 2.5 weeks of treatment, compared with 45 weeks and 72 weeks for inpatient hospitalization and home tutoring, respectively. This study has two important shortcomings, as we noted above: The children were not randomly assigned to each treatment, therefore results are heuristic only; in addition, it does not include a control group who remained untreated and the efficacy of treatment cannot be judged.

Very recently, Mansdorf and Lukens (1987) described the use of a cognitive-behavioral approach to the treatment of anxiety-based school refusal. Although not a group study, the treatment orientation utilized will be described in detail because of its innovative features. Subjects included two children (a 10-year-old boy and a 12-year-old girl) described by the authors as separation-anxious school phobics. Both children previously had failed to respond to treatment with imipramine hydrochloride. Pre-treatment assessment consisted of delineating maladaptive self-statements and beliefs for both the parents and the children as well as determining already existing consequences for attendance or nonattendance at school. Intervention included self-instructional training for the children, cognitive restructuring for the parents, and environmental restructuring in which parental reinforcement was made contingent on school attendance and children were gradually exposed to the school setting. The cognitive training for both the children and parents was aimed at promoting the use of coping cognitions. For example, one of the children reported a concern that "the kids in school make fun of me." This inhibiting position was replaced with the following coping cognition. "That's their problem, not mine." The parents of this child reported a concern that "my child is sick so I shouldn't push." This inhibiting cognition was replaced by the following coping cognition: "This is the way to help."

The authors report that within four weeks both children were able to remain alone at school all day. Further, at three-month follow-up, treatment gains were maintained. Although this study obviously is in need of replication with a larger sample and longer follow-up, it provides a promising approach to providing cognitive and behavioral treatment procedures for both the school-refusing child and his or her parents.

Although relatively good outcome has been achieved using a variety of behavioral interventions in the treatment of anxiety-based school refusal, literature in this area is plagued by a number of methodological problems. First, there is a relative paucity of controlled group comparisons studies that evaluate the relative efficacy of different treatment procedures. Second, researchers in this area have failed to adequately describe their samples, perhaps, most importantly, in terms of their diagnostic composition (i.e., separation anxiety disorder or phobic disorder of school). Third, most of the treatment studies conducted to date have failed to utilize objective, standardized assessment procedures and thus have been unable to measure treatment outcome in a reliable and valid manner.

In reviewing the literature on the behavioral treatment of school refusers, it is clear that return to school is perhaps the most important measure of outcome. In attempting to achieve this outcome, there are two behavioral methods that have been most frequently employed:

graduated in vivo exposure and in vivo flooding. In vivo flooding, which essentially consists of rapid forced reentry to school, has been described as the preferred treatment technique by a number of authors, including Kennedy (1965) who reports success with this intervention with Type I school refusers. The group comparison study by Blagg and Yule (1984), already described also successfully employed this treatment technique. Alternatively, other individuals working in this area have favored a gradual return to school using graduated in vivo exposure or in vivo desensitization procedures (e.g., Last & Francis, 1988). While the literature and our clinical experience indicate that both procedures (flooding and graduated exposure) are successful in achieving reentry, it should be noted that flooding often has the advantage of a more immediate return to school (i.e., three days for flooding versus eight to twelve weeks for graduated exposure), while the graduated approach has the advantage of circumventing the dropout problem that frequently occurs when using flooding procedures.

Imipramine hydrochloride (see pharmacotherapy, below), often has been used in conjunction with behavioral intervention in the treatment of anxiety-based school refusal. For example, we have found the drug to be a useful adjunct to behavioral treatment, particularly in very chronic and intractable cases, and also in cases where panic is of extreme proportions. The authors' common clinical practice is to add imipramine as an adjunct to behavior therapy after initial attempts at behavior therapy have failed (usually determined after a 2-week period). Interestingly, recent preliminary data in the authors' work suggest that imipramine may be equally effective in children who have separation anxiety or a truly phobic disorder of school.

Currently, Last and colleagues are investigating the utility of imipramine as an adjunct to behavioral treatment in a controlled double-blind study. All of the children participating in this study received a behavioral treatment package consisting of graduated in vivo exposure, coping self-statement training for the child, and cognitive restructuring for the parents. Each participating child is randomly assigned to receive either imipramine or a placebo. In an attempt to address some of the methodological concerns raised above, in addition to main treatment condition comparisons, results will be analyzed according to the diagnostic status of the children, that is, separation-anxious or phobic of school. Moreover, multiple, objective standardized outcome measures are included to help improve assessment of outcome in this study.

Overanxious Disorder

Unfortunately, no reports on the treatment of overanxious children have appeared in the literature to date. From our clinical experience, we have found a combined cognitive-behavioral treatment package consisting of relaxation training, exposure, and cognitive therapy to be the most successful treatment approach. In this way, the physiological, behavioral, and cognitive components of the disorder are addressed. A similar approach currently is being used by other clinical researchers for the treatment of this disorder (Kendall, personal communication).

Avoidant Disorder

Similar to overanxious disorder, the treatment of avoidant disorder has not yet been described in the literature. We have been treating the disorder with social skills training in a group setting. In some cases of avoidant disorder, anxiety appears to stem from the children's lack of social skills necessary for interacting effectively with unfamiliar people; other children have an excessive level of anxiety that interferes with their ability to utilize the skills that they have already acquired. In administering social skills training, both types of avoidant cases can be treated successfully, since the treatment teaches skills and simultaneously enforces graduated exposure. In addition, the use of cognitive techniques have proven to be helpful in some cases, particularly for those children who have high levels of anticipatory anxiety.

Obsessive-Compulsive Disorder

There have been a few published reports describing the behavioral treatment of obsessive-compulsive disorder in children. As in the adult literature on obsessive-compulsive disorder, response prevention has been the most common and perhaps the most successful behavioral intervention utilized with this population. Several case reports and one multiple-case series have described the successful application of response prevention to ritualistic behavior (Bolton, Collins, & Steinberg, 1983; Mills, Agras, Barlow, & Mills, 1973; Ong & Leng, 1979; Stanley, 1980; Zikis, 1983).

Utilizing a single case design, Mills, Agras, Barlow, and Mills (1973) treated ritualistic behaviors in a 14-year-old boy with response prevention. The patient performed a set of complicated and time-consuming rituals at bedtime and on awakening in the morning. The night rituals included repeatedly checking the placement of his pillow and folding and unfolding his pajamas before putting them on. Morning rituals included the laying out of his clothes in a particular manner and dressing in a specified and rigid order. Following a 12-day baseline, response prevention first was implemented for the night rituals. The night rituals were successfully decreased in this manner and simultaneously an immediate reduction and continuous decline was noted in the morning rituals as well during the 10-day treatment phase. Following the treatment phase, return to baseline showed no further occurrence of night or morning rituals.

Stanley (1980) utilized response prevention to treat the rituals of an 8-year-old girl. Rituals included repetitive nighttime behaviors (for example, fluffing her pillow three times before getting undressed at night, going to the bathroom three times before going to bed, etc.). Response prevention resulted in the elimination of rituals within a 2-week period, with no reoccurrences reported at 1-year follow-up. Similarly, Zikis (1983) successfully treated an 11-year-old girl with seven separate rituals within a 1-week period.

Ong and Leng (1979) applied response prevention in conjunction with other behavioral techniques (participant modeling, DRO) and pharmacotherapy (diazepam) in the treatment of a 13-year-old girl with washing rituals. Although the child was reported to have improved, it is not possible for this study to determine the relative effectiveness of the different treatment components administered since they all were received concurrently.

In a multiple-case series report, Bolton, Collins, and Steinberg (1983) described the treatment of 15 adolescents with obsessive-compulsive rituals. Response prevention was used to decrease compulsive ritualizing, which primarily consisted of checking and/or cleaning. Results showed good outcome, with symptoms being relieved entirely or reduced to a mildly incapacitating level in most cases. In addition treatment gains were maintained at follow-up (9 to 48 months) in the majority of cases. Two investigators have reported the use of extinction procedures for eliminating compulsive reassurance-seeking behavior (Francis, 1988; Hallam, 1974). Hallam (1974) reported on a 15-year-old girl who displayed persistent questioning concerning her personal appearance, the truth of factual statements, and the implications of supposedly unkind remarks. The child was treated on an inpatient unit using extinction procedures, where personnel were instructed to respond to her request for reassurance by answering "I can't answer that," or "that is a ritual question." Hallam reports that following 1 week of treatment, questioning had been dramatically reduced from a estimated frequency between 50 and 100 times a day to 17 at the end of the week. Francis (1988) also described the successful application of an extinction procedure for reducing reassurance-seeking verbalizations. The patient was a 10-year-old boy who repeatedly questioned his parents about his physical health and the possibility of his dying. Utilizing an ABAB single-case design, extinction procedures were shown to be effective in eliminating the maladaptive behavior.

The involvement of family members is a major consideration in the treatment of childhood obsessive-compulsive disorder. Almost all of the behavior treatment reports to date have included family participation, either as observers or co-therapists. Family involvement in treatment was maximized in a multiple-case report conducted by Queiroz, Motta, Madi, Sossai, and Boren (1981). Functional analysis of the case of a 9-year-old boy exhibiting multiple compulsions revealed that the compulsions were maintained by the behavior of the mother, who was also ritualistic and contingently attended to the child's display of compulsions. The treatment plan was implemented by the family and included several components, such as extinction of maternal attention for maladaptive behaviors, the development of alternative responses, and a home-based token system with a response course cost feature to reinforce the alternative behaviors. Unfortunately, no data is presented for this case, although the treatment was considered to be successful. In a second case the multiple obsessive-compulsive rituals of a 12-year-old girl were modified through changing family reinforcement patterns. In this case, parents were asked to report on a weekly basis the number of ritualistic behaviors observed. After 88 weeks of treatment, all of the ritualistic behaviors had been eliminated, according to the parents monitoring reports.

Summary

From the above brief summary of the state-of-the-art in the behavioral treatment of childhood anxiety disorders, it is clear that extensive research is necessary in order to clearly determine the treatment of choice for these disorders. However, in the absence of such investigations we have made some suggestions based on the available literature and our clinical experience. Below is a case history of a separation-anxious child who was treated successfully with behavioral intervention.

Case Study: Separation Anxiety Disorder

Kenny is a 10-year-old boy who was brought to the Child and Adolescent Anxiety Disorder Clinic at Western Psychiatric Institute and Clinic by his parents. Kenny's parents reported that he is extremely fearful of going to school and has refused to go for the past several months. In addition to school refusal, Kenny is unable to enter all other situations that involve him being separated from his parents, for example, playing in the backyard or at other children's homes, going to Little League practice, staying home with the babysitter, and so on. When pushed to go to school, or to be separated from his parents when at home, Kenny responds with crying and tantrums. He also has threatened to hurt himself (e.g., jump out of the classroom window) if forced to go to school.

Kenny's separation problems began about 1 year prior to his evaluation at the clinic. At that time Kenny's father was having problems with alcohol, and was frequently absent from the home for prolonged periods of time. Kenny's separation anxiety worsened gradually over the course of the year, resulting in complete school refusal. Help had been sought at a local mental health clinic where psychotherapy was provided, but Kenny continued to deteriorate. He developed significant depressive symptomatology, including dysphoric mood, guilty feelings about his problems, occasional wishes to be dead, and periodic early morning awakening.

Kenny and his parents individually were administered a semi-structured diagnostic interview schedule. Results from the interviews confirmed the diagnosis of separation anxiety disorder, according to DSM-III criteria. More specifically, Kenny met the following DSM-III criteria for separation anxiety disorder: (1) worry about harm befalling his mother and father (e.g., "they'll be in an accident"), (2) worries about being kidnapped and separated from his parents, (3) somatic complaints when anticipating a separation situation, (4) excessive distress on separation, and (5) refusal to be alone at home or stay at home with the babysitter. Although Kenny also had significant depressive symptomatology, these symptoms were seen as secondary to his primary anxiety condition and were not numerous enough to meet criteria for a DSM-III diagnosis of major depression. It was anticipated that his depressive symptoms would remit as his separation anxiety improved.

Graduated in vivo exposure was selected as the treatment for this patient. This treatment approach previously has yielded positive results with a variety of childhood and adult anxiety disorders, particularly where avoidance behavior is a central feature of the disorder. It was explained to the patient and his parents that the only way in which Kenny would overcome his fear was by repeatedly confronting the very situations that he feared and avoided. It was further emphasized that these situations would be tackled in a very gradual manner beginning with tasks that caused little or no anxiety and then, in a stepwise manner, moving to increasingly difficult tasks. Kenny was told that he would be in control of the rate at which he would proceed, and that he never would be asked to do anything that he did not think he was ready for.

Using the above approach, Kenny's school avoidance was tackled first. After 6 weeks of treatment, Kenny was attending half-days of school on a regular basis. At this time, it appeared that his progress with school generalized to other nonschool-related separation situations. During the next six sessions, Kenny continued to work toward attending full days of school and also worked on home-related separation situations using the same graduated exposure approach. He continued to make consistent progress and showed no signs of separation anxiety by the end of 3 months of weekly treatment sessions.

The above child represents an excellent responder, who reached a level of comfort that cannot be expected on a regular basis. Many children improve greatly, as manifested by reductions in avoidance, but retain various degrees of discomfort during separation or in anticipation of it.

PHARMACOLOGICAL TREATMENTS

Historically, pharmacological intervention in children has followed the practice established with adults, in order to avoid using compounds in children until their deleterious effects are fairly well understood from previous experience with adults so that treatments used in children follow established usage in adults. This approach is eminently sensible. There has been also a long-held practice of treating anxiety symptoms rather than anxiety syndromes. Because anxiety symptoms occur in a wide variety of psychiatric disorders, a diversity of childhood conditions have been treated for the relief of anxiety. This clinical literature dates back to the late 1950s and early 1960s. It is not summarized here because it has little if any relevance to the management of childhood or adolescent anxiety disorders today (it is reviewed elsewhere [Gittelman-Klein, 1978; Klein, in press]). Suffice it to say that the compounds investigated included neuroleptics, psychostimulants, antihistamines, and anxiolytics (anti-anxiety agents). Only the latter have remained as warranting consideration in the psychopharmacological management of anxiety disorders of young age. As is the case of the behavioral treatments, the rest of the studies, although markedly superior to the early ones, have not relied on diagnostic concepts consistent with the current nomenclature for identifying patient groups. The authors have attempted to organize the clinical material to fit the DSM-III-R classification, but the fit is rarely perfect.

Separation Anxiety Disorder

Of all the childhood anxiety disorders, separation anxiety disorder has been the one that has received the most attention with regard to pharmacological treatment. The first drug trial was based on a hypothesis linking childhood separation anxiety to adult panic and agoraphobic disorder. Klein observed that a large proportion of these patients had a childhood history of severe separation anxiety and that their response to initial panic in adulthood had been clinging dependent behavior. Other reports have yielded similar findings (Gittelman & Klein, 1985). Klein (1964) reasoned that agoraphobic adults perhaps experienced a dysregulation of the ethologically adaptive biological processes that regulate anxiety commonly triggered by separation (this notion is one of few applications of evolutionary theory to human psychopathology discussed in Chapter 1). Klein hypothesized that panic anxiety might be a pathological manifestation of normal separation anxiety and, since imipramine relieved adult panic attacks, it should be useful in children with separation anxiety if the two conditions shared a common pathophysiology. An initial open clinical trial with imipramine was conducted in children with school phobia, since their phobic disorder is so often the consequence of pathological separation anxiety. In an open clinical trial the drug seemed helpful, since 85% of severe and chronic school phobic children returned to school (Rabiner & Klein, 1969). A placebo-controlled 6-week study of imipramine in 7 to 15 year olds who were unable to attend school regularly was conducted subsequently (Gittelman-Klein & Klein, 1971, 1973, 1980). In all but three cases of the 45 children who participated, the presence of separation anxiety was ascertained. Imipramine (mean of 150 mg/day) was significantly superior to placebo in several functional domains such as in inducing school return and other aspects of anxious symptomatology, such as fear and physical symptoms before attending school. Depressive symptoms also improved, but the presence of depression was not necessary for reduction of anxiety to occur, so that children benefited from the medication regardless of whether depression was present. This finding is important in view of the diagnostic overlap between anxiety and depression discussed in Chapter 2.

Berney, Kolvin, Bhate, Garside, Jeans, Kay, and Scarth (1981) investigated the efficacy of clomipramine in doses of 40 to 75 mg in school phobic children, many of whom suffered from separation anxiety and depression. There was no greater improvement in the medication group compared with the placebo group. Both treatment groups demonstrated relatively low levels of improvement at the end of the 12-week treatment. For example, almost half of the children were still not attending school on their own, and a substantial proportion still had significant levels of separation anxiety. Several factors may be responsible for the contrasting results in the two studies that used tricyclics of similar potency. As Berney et al. note, the clomipramine dose used was lower than the imipramine dose used by Gittelman-Klein and Klein (1973), who had reported that at least 75 mg per day was necessary for improvement to occur. Different clinical sample characteristics or the kind of psychotherapy given to the children could also have contributed to the discrepancies between the two studies. These methodological differences are improbable since the placebo effects were very similar in the two reports. In the absence of studies that indicate the dosages at which clomipramine seems effective, the results of the study are unfortunately ambiguous.

The pattern of results in the study by Berney et al. (1981) provides interesting information concerning the course of symptomatology over time. The investigators undertook careful assessment of the clinical changes over the course of the trial. Because the two treatment groups did not differ in their response, the results for both groups are pooled. Before treatment, 87% of the children were rated as having significant levels of separation anxiety, and 44% were judged as having levels of depression of similar clinical severity. After 4 weeks of treatment 68% still had separation anxiety, whereas only 12% were still depressed. The patter of clinical outcome argues against the view that separation anxiety when it is accompanied by clinical depression represents a primary depressive state. The marked improvement of depression after the first 4 weeks of treatment although separation anxiety continued is consistent with the anxiety disorder being primary in these school phobic children.

Because the children who entered the authors' study of imipramine were selected for the presence of school phobia rather than separation anxiety disorder per se, the authors planned a further investigation of the drug in children with DSM-III separation anxiety disorder, and who had an array of behavioral difficulties. Children could have sleep difficulties, problems separating in situations outside of school such as playing away from home, being unable to stay home without their parents, or being uncomfortable when parents went out as a result of separation anxiety. In other words, children were selected for separation anxiety disorder and not school phobia. A total of 20 children, ages 6 to 15, 4 of whom had school phobia and 16 of whom had separation anxiety disorder but no school phobia, completed a 6-week trial of imipramine (N = 11) or placebo (N = 9). The mean final daily dose was 153 mg. No advantage for imipramine over the placebo was obtained on any of the measures of clinical status. The overall improvement rate with the drug was only 50%, identical to the placebo improvement rate (Klein, unpublished [a]).

Unfortunately, the sample is too small to permit definitive conclusions regarding the efficacy of imipramine in this study. However, there is little question that the clinical impact of the tricyclic in this trial was not nearly as impressive as it had been in the earlier study. We conclude that the role of tricyclics for the relief of separation anxiety disorder is questionable.

Bernstein, Garfinkel, and Borchardt (1987) also treated a small group of school phobic children (7 - 17 years) with imipramine in doses of 3 mg/kd/d or placebo for 8 weeks. They report some superiority for imipramine; on the drug five out of the seven children returned to school (71%), whereas two out of five (40%) did so on placebo. No statistical differences between the treatments were obtained. The diagnostic composition was mixed, consisting of either DSM-III anxiety or depressive disorders. The small number of cases treated precludes meaningful treatment contrasts, and the lack of diagnostic purity would confound the clinical interpretation of the results, even if a larger sample were obtained.

The investigation by Bernstein et al. (1987), of imipramine and placebo also included a group treated with alprazolam, a relatively recent benzodiazepine. Of the seven children on alprazolam, six returned to school (86%) versus two of five (40%) on placebo. No measure showed a significant advantage for the drug over the placebo, but as noted, the sample is too small to permit meaningful contrasts. In our clinical experience, which is limited so far to only 18 youngsters (6 - 17 years old, mean 11) with separation anxiety disorder refractory to psychotherapy, alprazolam was effective over a 6-week period in daily doses of 0.5 to 6.0 mg/day, mean 1.9 mg (Klein, unpublished data [b]). Parents and psychiatrists judged over 80% as being improved to a significant degree, whereby children rated themselves improved in 65% of the cases.

A pilot study of a standard benzodiazepine, diazepam (Valium), in 15 children with separation anxiety disorder was planned. However, the trial was abandoned after treating five children because the medication led to marked behavioral disinhibition in several instances, without evidence of positive clinical efficacy.

Alprazolam (Xanax) has been reported to be effective in adults with panic disorders (Ballenger et al., 1988). It has been conjectured that it may have clinical properties different from those of other members of the same class. At this time, there is no empirical basis for its use in children, since open clinical trials can only be suggestive. However, the side effect profile may be informative. Only one (5.5%) adolescent could not tolerate the medication because of drowsiness. Except for some drowsiness in two other children, side effects were very few and mild. Of greater importance is the fact that implementing .25 mg drug decrements every 3 to 4 days, no child showed withdrawal symptoms. This clinical observation seems to indicate that the recurrence of significant anxiety symptoms associated with alprazolam withdrawal in adults with panic disorder (Pecknold, Swinson, Kuch, & Lewis, 1988) does not occur with regularity in children or adolescents with separation anxiety disorder.

It has been recommended that anxiolytics not be used for longer than 6 weeks in children (Simeon & Ferguson, 1985); however, there is no empirical basis for this clinical dictum, and the authors' experience has failed to reveal untoward effects from more prolonged treatment. There does not appear to be any basis at this time on which to estimate the maximal treatment period, and there is no suggestive or known contraindication to more extended therapies.

Overanxious Disorder

Overanxious disorder of childhood or adolescence has been very poorly studied. As we discuss in Chapter 2, the clinical content is overinclusive and implicitly subsumes generalized social phobic disorders. One small open clinical trial of alprazolam (0.5 to 1.5 mg/d) has been reported in 12 youngsters between 7 and 17 years of age (Simeon & Ferguson, 1987). Significant amelioration of various symptomatologies, including anxiety, depression, and hyperactivity, was obtained after 4 weeks of treatment. Overall, 58% were judged improved. This rate of clinical improvement is difficult to assess in the absence of a treatment control, since no previous treatment studies have appeared that could suggest the expected level of improvement with a placebo. However, the heterogeneity of this diagnosis would make any investigation of treatment effect, even well controlled, difficult to interpret unambiguously. Would they apply to those with generalized social anxiety or to those with overanxiety unrelated to the social context?

Avoidant Disorder

As we have noted, the prevalence of avoidant disorder without concomitant psychopathology is not common among children referred for treatment. The clinical content overlaps considerably with the adult diagnosis of social phobia, generalized type. Depending on the clinician's predilection for using the child or adult section of the diagnostic manual, adolescents could be diagnosed as either avoidant or socially phobic. No psychopharmacological treatment studies have been conducted in social phobic adolescents. Current research with adults has found that drugs of the monoamine oxidase inhibitor class are effective in generalized social phobia (Liebowitz et al., 1986; Liebowitz et al., 1988). The adolescent and adult diagnoses probably represent the same syndrome; they appear to have the same clinical presentation and the adults treated for the disorder frequently have an adolescent onset. Therefore, it seems likely that pharmacological treatments found effective in socially phobic adults are applicable to similar adolescents.

Obsessive-Compulsive Disorder

Obsessive-compulsive disorder in a young age shares many characteristics with the adult form. Furthermore, as is the case with generalized social phobia, it is not unusual for adults to report an onset in childhood or adolescence. The hypothesis that the childhood and adult syndromes would have the same response to pharmacological treatment led to the treatment of children with medications previously found effective in adults. A preliminary report compared clomipramine, desmethylimipramine, and a placebo given in random order to eight youngsters with obsessive-compulsive disorder (mean age, 15.2 years). The maximum daily dose for both active agents was 150 mg/day. The drugs did not differ from the placebo or from each other (Rapoport, Elkins, & Mikkelsen, 1980). The final report of this study included 19 children, 10 to 18 years of age (mean, 14.5) (Flament et al., 1985). In this comparison, clomipramine and placebo only were contrasted; each condition lasted for a 5-week period in random order, with maximum daily doses of 200 mg (mean, 141 mg). Clomipramine treatment was significantly superior to the placebo on several measures of obsessive-compulsive symptomatology, with marked overall improvement reported in 75% of the cases. This finding parallels results reported for adult patients (Thoren, Asberg, Cronholm, Jornestedt, & Traskman, 1980). Treatment effectiveness was not associated with the presence of depression or with improvement of depression. In addition, plasma levels of drug metabolites were unrelated to improvement. In fact, there was a significant negative correlation between improvement on a scale of obsessive-compulsive symptoms and desmethylclomipramine levels.

To clarify the specificity of clomipramine, a further study compared it to another tricyclic, desipramine, in a cross-over study (Leonard et al., 1988). Twenty-one youngsters from 8 to 19 years of age received each compound for 5 weeks each. In this rigorous test of comparative efficacy between two drugs of the same class, clear superiority for clomipramine over desipramine was obtained.

The authors of these studies suggest that the CMI effect is mediated by serotonergic function. Before treatment, children with OCD did not differ from normals on measures of platelet serotonin levels, but improvement on the drug was highly and positively associated both with initial serotonin level, and with its reduction during exposure to the drug (Flament, Rapoport, Murphy, Berg, & Lake, 1987).

A new compound, fluoxatine, has been marketed in the United States since the beginning of 1988. It is reported to have significant clinical impact on adult obsessive-compulsive disorder. Studies in younger patients are ongoing and it is likely that favorable results will emerge.

Summary

There is limited evidence supporting the efficacy of drug treatment in anxiety disorders of childhood as a whole. The most consistent finding is for the efficacy of clomipramine in obsessive-compulsive children and adolescents. Early reports indicated that imipramine was effective in separation anxiety disorder, but the treatment may not have the impact originally found. Alprazolam, a recently developed benzo-diazepine, has received very little attention in children. Two open clinical trials have yielded encouraging results in separation anxiety and overanxious disorders. It is not clear that this compound has a place in the management of childhood and adolescent anxiety, but the withdrawal syndrome reported in adults has not been observed. The pharmacological treatment of avoidant disorder has not been attempted.

5

RISK FACTORS

The investigation of risk factors for psychiatric disorders provides valuable information for early detection and intervention, and, ultimately, for prevention. A substantial body of work currently exists on risk factors for anxiety disorder, and much of it has focused on children. Below, we summarize the published literature as it relates to the role of family factors, stressful life events, and developmental and hereditary factors, in the pathogenesis of childhood anxiety disorders.

FAMILIAL FACTORS

Whether there is a familial factor involved in the development of childhood anxiety disorders has been addressed by a number of investigations. One method for studying this question has been referred to as the "top-down" method, where the children of adult patients diagnosed as having an anxiety disorder are studied. The second method has been referred to as the "bottom-up" method, where parents and other relatives of children diagnosed as having anxiety disorders are studied. Investigations using both of these methods and their results will be described.

"Top-Down" Studies

Four studies have used the top-down method to assess anxiety disorders in children. Berg (1976) investigated the prevalence of school phobia in the children of agoraphobic women via a questionnaire survey. School phobia was assumed to have been present when mothers answered *yes* to this question: "Has the child ever completely refused to go to school for longer than 1 or 2 days since starting school at 7?" (p. 86). Results for children aged 7 to 15 years showed a prevalence rate of 7%. However, when children of secondary school age (11 to 15 years) were considered separately, the prevalence rate rose to 14%. Berg states that these rates (particularly for children 11 to 15 years) are higher than what would be expected in the general population.

Interpretation of findings for this study are hampered by several methodological problems: (1) the criterion for identifying cases of school phobia is overinclusive, as cases of depression, medical illness, and truancy may meet the criterion and result in misclassification as school phobia, although it is less likely for truancy to be misclassified as school phobia since truants do not resist going to school (they leave for school willingly, but never get there), (2) lack of a psychopathological control group renders one unable to determine whether the rates of school phobia observed are due to psychopathology per se, rather than agoraphobia specifically, and (3) lack of a matched normal control group precludes comparison of obtained rates with base rates for the general population.

In a similar but smaller study, Buglass, Clarke, Henderson, Kreitman, and Presley (1977) compared the offspring of 30 agoraphobic women with the offspring of 30 matched nonpsychiatrically disturbed women. Information on the children was obtained through interviewing of the mothers and a symptom checklist. Results indicated that the two groups did not differ in the rate of psychiatric illness in general, or school phobia in particular. In fact, contrary to expectation, none of the agoraphobics' children showed agoraphobia or school refusal.

Unfortunately, the investigations did not report the number of offspring in different age brackets. Since school phobia has been shown to yield a higher prevalence rate in preadolescence and adolescence, rather than early or middle childhood (e.g., Berg, 1976; Last, Francis, Hersen, Kazdin, & Strauss, 1987), such information is of importance. As noted by Gittelman (1986), it is possible for no case of school phobia to occur in a very small sample if the expected rate is relatively low (e.g., 10 - 15%) (p. 114). Moreover, the use of the family history method — where the children themselves were not interviewed directly — most probably resulted in an underestimate of psychiatric illness in this study.

Weissman, Leckman, Merikangas, Gammon, and Prusoff (1984) compared children of women with major depression with or without a history of anxiety disorders and a group of matched control subjects. The family history method was used, where information on the children's psychiatric status was obtained from the proband, spouse, and other first-degree relatives. The depressed probands with concurrent anxiety disorders were divided into three groups: (1) depression and agoraphobia, (2) depression and panic disorder, and (3) depression and generalized anxiety disorder. The anxiety groups then were compared with women who had depression but no anxiety disorder and normals.

Results were summarized in Table 5.1. As can be observed, an increased risk of anxiety disorders, specifically, separation anxiety disorder, was present in the children of women with depression and panic disorder, with 11 of 19 (36.8%) offspring meeting DSM-III criteria for the diagnosis. None of the offspring of normal or depressed only probands met criteria for separation anxiety disorder. In the other two depression plus anxiety disorder groups, relatively low rates were obtained for separation anxiety disorder, with 2 of 18 (11.1%) children of agoraphobic probands and 2 of 32 (6.3%) children of generalized anxiety disorder women meeting diagnostic criteria. When the offspring of agoraphobic and panic disorder women are combined, the risk of separation anxiety disorder decreased to 24.3%, a rate still greater than in the other groups.

Although these data are important, it should be noted that use of the family history method, where the offspring have not been interviewed directly, most probably resulted in an underestimation of the rate of psychopathology. Therefore, the study addresses the *relative* rate of separation anxiety disorder in the children of the groups studied, but not the expected rates. The possible effect of comorbid major depression in the mothers cannot be evaluated since the children of patients with anxiety disorders only were not included in the study (such studies are ongoing in several centers). It should be emphasized that an increased rate of anxiety disorders *only* was obtained in the children of patients with panic disorder. Agoraphobia and generalized anxiety disorder did not result in a higher morbid risk for offspring. The reason for this is unclear, at least for agoraphobia, given previous research findings supporting a relationship between panic disorder and agoraphobia. Indeed, DSM-III-R now considers the two illnesses to be variants of the same disorder (American Psychiatric Association, 1987). However, the number of mothers with agoraphobia was small and was probably insufficient to yield firm results.

Turner, Beidel, and Costello (1987) directly assessed children of anxiety disordered patients. These children were compared with children of patients with dysthymic disorder, children of normal parents, and normal school children. All children were assessed with a semi-structured interview schedule and diagnosed according to DSM-III. Results indicated that of 16 children of anxiety disorder probands, 6 (38%)

TABLE 5.1

Anxiety Disorders in the Offspring of Normal, Depressed Only,
and Depressed and Anxious Probands

Proband Group	No. of Children at Risk	Any Anxiety Disorder		Separation Anxiety Disorder	
		%	n	%	n
Normal	87	2.3	2	0.0	0
Depression, no anxiety disorder	38	0.0	0	0.0	0
Depression plus agoraphobia	18	11.1	2	11.1	2
Depression plus panic	19	36.8	7	36.8	7
Depression plus GAD	32	6.3	2	6.3	2
Depression plus agoraphobia/panic	37	24.3	9	24.3	9

NOTE: From "Depression and Anxiety Disorders in Parents and Children," by M. M. Weissman, J. F. Leckman, K. R. Merikangas, G. D. Gammon, and B. A. Prusoff 1984, *Archives of General Psychiatry*, *41*, pp. 847–949. Copyright © 1984, American Medical Association.

received a diagnosis of an anxiety disorder, 4 of the children met criteria for separation anxiety disorder, and 2 met criteria for overanxious disorder. By comparison, 3 of the 14 offspring (21%) of dysthymic disorder patients met diagnostic criteria for an anxiety disorder, including one child with separation anxiety disorder, one with overanxious disorder, and one with social phobia. Only one child of the normal parents and none of the normal school children met criteria for an anxiety disorder diagnosis. Statistical analysis of the data indicated that the anxiety disorders group significantly differed from both normal control groups, but not from the dysthymic disorder group.

The above results were obtained by the inclusion of multiple offspring of same parents. Turner et al. (1987) reanalyzed their data with a reduced sample, randomly selecting only one child from each of the families with multiple children. Reanalysis with the reduced sample replicated the full sample results, with 6 of 13 offspring (46%) in the anxiety disorders group meeting criteria for an anxiety disorder (4 with separation anxiety and 2 with overanxious disorder), 3 of 11 dysthymic offspring (27%) meeting diagnostic criteria for an anxiety disorder (1 with overanxious disorder, 1 with separation anxiety disorder, and

1 with social phobia), and no children in the solicited normal or school normal groups meeting diagnostic criteria.

Although Turner et al. (1987) were able to demonstrate an increased risk of anxiety disorders in the children of anxiety disordered patients compared with the two nonpatient groups, they were not able to demonstrate differences between the two patient groups. The selection of dysthymic disorder probands as the psychopathological control group for the study may be problematic in that a relationship between affective and anxiety disorders has been suggested by previous research. Therefore, studies with more power (i.e., larger samples) are necessary to investigate the issue.

"Bottom-Up" Studies

A number of bottom-up studies have been conducted where the relatives of child patients with anxiety disorders have been evaluated. Berg, Butler, and Pritchard (1974) evaluated maternal psychiatric illness in school phobic adolescents admitted to an inpatient psychiatric unit. Maternal psychiatric history of 100 school phobic youngsters were compared with maternal histories of 113 hospitalized nonschool phobic patients. Maternal psychiatric illness was evaluated by examining hospital and medical records. One-fifth of the mothers in both groups had a history of some type of psychiatric disturbance. Of these approximately one-half were diagnosed as having an affective disorder, which was defined in this study as anxiety, depression, or phobias. Thus, maternal psychiatric illness in the two patient groups did not significantly differ. Obviously, the use of record review as opposed to direct interviews severely hampers conclusions that can be drawn from this investigation. Moreover, the lumping together of affective and anxiety disorders under the category of "affective disorders" limits interpretation of findings.

Gittelman-Klein (1975) interviewed the parents of 42 school phobic and 42 hyperactive children to determine their psychiatric histories. Results were analyzed for three specific diagnostic categories: major depression, specific phobias, and separation anxiety disorder. No differences appeared between the two groups of parents for major depression or specific phobias. However, the parents of school phobic youngsters were found to have a significantly higher rate of separation anxiety disorder than parents of hyperactive children (19% vs. 2%, respectively).

In addition to the above, parents reported on siblings' histories of psychiatric illness, particularly school phobia. Among 67 siblings of the school phobic children, 11 (16%) had a clear-cut history of school phobia. In contrast, none of 66 siblings of hyperactive probands were reported to have a history of school phobia. These differences between the two groups were statistically significant. Interestingly, when the relationship between parental separation anxiety disorder and school phobia in siblings was examined, it was found that separation anxiety in the parents was not correlated with the presence of school phobia in the siblings. Interpretation of findings from this investigation are hampered by several ambiguities. First, diagnostic criteria for school phobia and separation anxiety disorder are not reported. Second, a related question concerns why separation anxiety disorder was examined in the parents while school phobia was examined in the siblings. Finally, although interviewers were unaware of the questions investigated, they were not blind to the children's diagnostic status, which potentially could seriously bias results.

Last, Phillips, and Statfeld (1987) examined the prevalence of two childhood anxiety disorders — separation anxiety and overanxious disorders — in the mothers of children diagnosed as having one or both of these disorders, and a control group of mothers who were psychiatrically disturbed but did not have an anxiety or affective disorder. DSM-III diagnostic criteria were used to diagnose both the children and their mothers. The diagnoses of the mothers' childhood disorders were conducted blindly through the use of a structured diagnostic questionnaire ("Childhood History Questionnaire") by raters who were unaware of the children's disorders. The study was designed to determine whether there is a relationship between mothers and their children for childhood anxiety disorders, and whether the nature of this relationship is general or specific. It was hypothesized that a specific relationship would exist, that is: (1) mothers of children with separation anxiety disorder had separation anxiety disorder as children, and (2) mothers of overanxious children had overanxious disorder as children.

Results indicated that only one of the two hypotheses was supported. No differences were found in the rates of separation anxiety disorder for the three groups of mothers. In contrast, the rate of overanxious disorder was significantly higher in mothers of overanxious children than in mothers of either separation anxious children or control children. More specifically, in the overanxious disorder group, 18 of 43 mothers (42%) reported a childhood history of overanxious disorder, compared to 2 of 21 mothers (9.5%) in the separation anxiety disorder group, and 5 of 33 mothers (15%) in the control group.

While data from this study supported a specific relationship between overanxious disorder in mothers and their children, such a relationship was not shown for separation anxiety disorder. These findings are contrasting to those reported from Gittelman-Klein (1975). It is possible that the method of assessment utilized in the Last, Phillips, and Statfeld study obscured a relationship for separation anxiety disorder. Separation anxiety disorder symptoms, as compared to those present in overanxious disorder, generally are more specific and of a shorter duration, with DSM-III requiring only a 2-week duration for the diagnosis. Direct interviews with the mothers rather than a symptom checklist might have helped to probe for the more specific and relatively transient symptoms of separation anxiety disorder.

In a bottom-up study conducted by Livingston, Nugent, Rader, and Smith (1985), the relatives of 12 anxious and 11 depressed children were examined using the family history method. Relatives primarily included mothers, fathers, and grandparents, yielding a sample size of 69 in the anxiety disorder group and 58 in the depressed group. Results indicated that in most respects the family histories of the two groups did not differ. Strikingly, only one relative in each of the groups was diagnosed as having an anxiety disorder.

As the investigators themselves noted, their study must be considered in light of methodological limitations, including the small number of probands included and use of the family history method to diagnose psychiatric illness. In concluding their paper, they stated that large scale family studies are needed with instruments utilized that are sensitive to detecting anxiety disorders.

Another small study (Bernstein & Garfinkel, 1988) examined psychopathology in the first-degree relatives of six children with school phobia using the family study method. Familial psychopathology in the school phobic families was compared to rates obtained in five families of children with other psychiatric disorders. Results indicated that 7 of 12 (58%) parents of school phobic children showed an anxiety disorder as compared to 3 of 10 (30%) parents of psychiatric controls. For siblings, 5 of 10 (50%) met criteria for an anxiety disorder in the school phobic group compared to none of 5 (0%) siblings in the control group. Unfortunately, the findings from this study may be regarded only as preliminary given the very small number of probands included in the school phobic and control groups (6 and 5, respectively).

Last, Hersen, Kazdin, Francis, and Grubb (1987) utilized the family study method to compare maternal psychiatric illness for children with separation anxiety disorder and/or overanxious disorder (n = 58) and for children who were psychiatrically disturbed but did not manifest an anxiety or affective disorder (n = 15). Mothers were interviewed directly about lifetime psychiatric illness with a semi-structured diagnostic interview and diagnosed according to DSM-III criteria. Interviewers were blind to children's diagnoses, and diagnostic agreement was evaluated by having a second clinician, also blind to children's diagnoses, independently score audiotapes of the interviews. Children in the control group were diagnosed as having behavior disorders, including conduct disorder, attention deficit disorder, and/or oppositional disorder.

Results indicated that mothers of children with anxiety disorders had a significantly higher lifetime rate of anxiety disorders than mothers of control children (83% vs. 40%, respectively). Moreover, when current rates of anxiety disorders were examined, the mothers of anxiety disordered children once again showed a significantly higher rate than the mothers of control children (57% vs. 20%, respectively).

Findings from the study are striking in that the vast majority of mothers of this clinic sample of anxiety disordered children showed a lifetime history of anxiety disorder. Moreover, approximately one-half of these mothers presented with an anxiety disorder at the same time their children were seen for similar problems. However, since mothers alone were interviewed, it is unclear whether the relationship for anxiety disorders is specific to the mother-child dyad or is indicative of a more general pattern of familial aggregation. The authors call for large scale family studies of this population in order to address this question.

Last, Hersen, Kazdin, Orvaschel, and Ye (1988) are conducting a large scale family study of childhood anxiety disorders. Lifetime psychiatric illness is assessed in the first- and second-degree relatives of child probands diagnosed as having an anxiety disorder. Data from the first year of this family study are now available and will be described in detail below.

Probands included 52 children with an anxiety disorder, a psychopathological control group of 40 children with attention deficit hyperactivity disorder (ADHD), and a normal control group of 54 children who had never been psychiatrically ill. All probands were required to be currently residing with at least one biological parent. In addition, inclusion criteria for anxiety disorder probands required a current

DSM-III-R diagnosis of an anxiety disorder and no current or past history of attention deficit hyperactivity disorder. ADHD probands were required to receive a current DSM-III-R diagnosis of attention deficit hyperactivity disorder and no current or past history of an anxiety or affective disorder. Finally, never psychiatrically ill probands, recruited from the community, were required to have no current or past history of any psychiatric disorder, as well as no current or past history of mental health contact. Probands in the never psychiatrically ill group were matched for age (within one year) and sex to the anxiety disorder probands.

All children in the study were administered a modified version of the *Schedule for Affective Disorders and Schizophrenia for School-Age Children* (present episode) (K-SADS-P: Puig-Antich & Chambers, 1978). This version of the K-SADS-P was modified by Last (1986) to include comprehensive sections on all DSM-III-R anxiety disorders. In addition, the modified interview schedule uses rating scales based on DSM-III-R criteria and covers past as well as current psychopathology. The modified interview was administered to parents and their children by a child clinical psychologist. Interrater diagnostic agreement was obtained for 61 of the 146 probands (42%) by having a second interviewer score audiotapes of the interviews. Diagnostic agreement for specific anxiety disorder diagnoses was 88% (n = 34). Agreement for attention deficit hyperactivity disorder (n = 27) and no psychiatric disorder (n = 12) was 100%. The diagnostic composition of the anxiety disorder group included: 10 with overanxious disorder, 9 with separation anxiety disorder, 8 with social phobia, 8 with simple phobia, 7 with obsessive-compulsive disorder, 3 with posttraumatic stress disorder, and 3 with avoidant disorder.

First-degree relatives (mothers, fathers, and full siblings, 5 years of age or older) were interviewed directly using the family study method. Adult first-degree relatives (18 years of age or older) were interviewed for current and past psychiatric illness with the *Structured Clinical Interview for DSM-III-R* (SCID: Spitzer, Williams, & Gibbon, 1986). Childhood disorders not contained in the SCID (e.g., separation anxiety disorder, overanxious disorder, avoidant disorder, and attention deficit hyperactivity disorder) also were administered to the adult relatives using sections from the modified K-SADS-P. Child and adolescent siblings of the probands were interviewed for current and past psychiatric illness with the modified K-SADS-P. Information on second-degree relatives (maternal and paternal grandparents, aunts, and uncles)

TABLE 5.2

Morbidity Risk for Anxiety Disorders in First- and Second-Degree
Relatives

		Proband Diagnosis			
	N	Anxiety (N=52)	N	ADHD (N=40)	N	Controls (N=54)
First-Degree	151	56.3[a,b]	103	41.5[c]	153	26.6
Second-Degree	447	21.1[d]	275	17.5[c]	496	12.1

NOTE: Rates are age corrected.
[a]vs. ADHD, $p < .10$
[b]vs. controls, $p < .0001$
[c]vs. controls, $p < .10$
[d]vs. controls, $p < .0005$

was obtained from the parents using the family history method. The
number of first-degree relatives included in the study were as follows:
151 in the anxiety disorder group, 103 in the ADHD group, and 153 in
the never psychiatrically ill group. Second-degree relatives included:
447 in the anxiety disorder group, 275 in the ADHD group, and 496 in
the never psychiatrically ill group.

All family interviews were conducted blindly. Interrater diagnostic
agreement was obtained by having a second interviewer score audiotapes of 25% of the family interviews. Diagnostic agreement was 98%
for specific anxiety disorder diagnoses (n = 65).

Age-adjusted morbidity risks for anxiety disorders in first- and
second-degree relatives can be observed in Table 5.2. As indicated, an
increased risk of anxiety disorders was found in the first- and second-
degree relatives of anxiety disorder probands compared with the relatives of controls. Differences between the first-degree relatives of
anxiety and ADHD probands, and ADHD and control probands, showed
trends ($p < .10$) in the expected direction.

Table 5.3 provides age-adjusted morbidity risks for anxiety disorders
by relationship and sex. As can be observed, the risk for female relatives
(mothers, sisters, and second-degree females) of anxiety probands and
ADHD probands were similar. Although the risk for female relatives
did not differ for the families of anxiety and ADHD probands, both
groups showed significantly higher morbidity risks for first-degree
female relatives compared to controls. These differences were due
primarily to differences obtained in the morbidity risks for mothers,
which for ill probands were at least twice that of controls.

TABLE 5.3
Morbidity Risk for Anxiety Disorders in First- and Second-Degree
Relatives By Relationship and Sex of Relative

	Proband Diagnosis		
	Anxiety (N = 52)	*ADHD* (N = 40)	*Controls* (N = 54)
Parents			
Fathers	51.4[a,b]	26.1	23.0
Mothers	74.1[c]	64.4[d]	31.3
Siblings			
Brothers	32.4[e]	0.0	8.3
Sisters	44.4	44.4	41.7
All 1st° Males	44.9[d,f]	19.4	18.8
All 1st° Females	68.7[g]	61.8[d]	34.1
All 2nd° Males	20.1[e,g]	12.5	8.2
All 2nd° Females	21.9	21.9	16.2

NOTE: Rates are age corrected.
[a]vs. ADHD, $p < .05$
[b]vs. controls, $p < .05$
[c]vs. controls, $p < .0005$
[d]vs. controls, $p < .01$
[e]vs. ADHD, $p < .10$
[f]vs. ADHD, $p < .01$
[g]vs. controls, $p < .005$

The risk for fathers and all first-degree male relatives was significantly higher in the families of anxiety probands than in the families of ADHD probands. A similar pattern emerged for brothers and second-degree male relatives, showing trends ($p < .10$) toward statistical significance. Comparison with the never psychiatrically ill control group showed the first- and second-degree male relatives of anxiety probands, but not ADHD probands, to be at increased risk.

Age-adjusted morbidity risks for specific anxiety disorder diagnoses in mothers is presented in Table 5.4. The morbidity risk for panic disorder (with or without agoraphobia) was higher in mothers of anxiety disorder probands compared to mothers of control probands. A similar trend was noted in comparison of the anxiety and ADHD groups. For social phobia, both patient groups showed significantly higher morbidity risks compared to the control group. Mothers in the anxiety group showed a higher morbidity risk for simple phobia compared to the other two groups. For generalized anxiety disorder, no statistically significant differences emerged. Similarly, no differences occurred in the rates of obsessive-compulsive disorder, although it should be noted that the

TABLE 5.4

Morbidity Risk for Anxiety Disorders in Mothers

| | Proband Diagnosis | | |
	Anxiety (N = 52)	*ADHD* (N = 40)	*Controls* (N = 54)
Panic disorder with or without agoraphobia	24.1	4.9	3.6
Social phobia	30.0	26.1	3.6
Simple phobia	32.8	22.2	10.5
Generalized anxiety disorder	3.8	14.0	7.1
Obsessive-compulsive disorder	7.5	0.0	0.0
Posttraumatic stress disorder	7.5	29.8	7.1
Separation anxiety disorder	12.0	7.7	5.8
Overanxious disorder	30.6	23.1	11.5
Avoidant disorder	16.0	10.3	3.7

NOTE: Rates are age corrected.

anxiety disorder group was the only group to identify cases with this diagnosis. The morbidity risk for posttraumatic stress disorder was significantly higher in the ADHD group than in the two other groups.

For childhood onset anxiety disorders, no statistically significant differences emerged for separation anxiety disorder, although risks were in the expected direction. In contrast, the anxiety disorder group had significantly higher rates of overanxious disorder and avoidant disorder than mothers in the control group. No differences emerged for the other pairwise comparisons for these two childhood disorders.

Although morbidity risks provide useful information, they give little indication about how anxiety disorders may segregate within families. To examine this factor, we used individual families as the unit of analysis and compared the three groups on the following: (1) number (percentage) of families where either the mother *or* father (or both) had an anxiety disorder, and (2) number (percentage) of families where *both* mother and father had an anxiety disorder. These data are presented in Table 5.5.

As indicated, the percentage of families having at least one parent with an anxiety disorder was in the expected direction (anxiety > ADHD > controls). Both patient groups significantly differed from the control group; differences between the anxiety and ADHD groups showed a trend toward statistical difference. Observing the percentage of families where *both* parents had an anxiety disorder, once again, findings were in the expected direction. However, the only statistically

TABLE 5.5

Segregation of Anxiety Disorders Within Families

	Proband Diagnosis		
	Anxiety (N = 52)	*ADHD* (N = 40)	*Controls* (N = 54)
Affected Family Members			
Father and/or mother	70.6	53.8	29.6
Both father and mother	13.7	5.1	0.0

NOTE: Rates are not age corrected.

significant difference emerged when comparing the anxiety and control groups.

In summary, findings from the first year of this family study showed a very high morbidity risk for anxiety disorders in the relatives of anxiety disordered children. Differences for the male relatives of this group compared with both the psychopathological and never psychiatrically ill control groups particularly were striking. For female relatives, meaningful differences were observed only for mothers, with mothers of anxiety disordered probands showing a greatly increased risk compared to mothers of never psychiatrically ill children. Interestingly, the risk for anxiety disorders in the mothers of anxiety probands and ADHD probands were comparable. However, when observing the specific *types* of anxiety disorders experienced by the two groups of mothers, differences emerged. Mothers of anxiety probands were more likely to receive diagnoses of panic disorders (panic disorder without agoraphobia, panic disorder with agoraphobia) than either the ADHD or never psychiatrically ill control groups. In contrast, mothers of ADHD probands were more likely than either of the other two groups of mothers to receive the diagnosis of posttraumatic stress disorder. Moreover, as children mothers of anxiety probands were more likely than mothers of control children to show childhood onset anxiety disorders, including overanxious disorder and avoidant disorder, while ADHD mothers were not. Finally, the segregation of anxiety disorders within individual families occurred most frequently in the anxiety disorder group.

Findings from the final sample obtained from this family study should continue to shed light on the familial nature of childhood anxiety disorders. In this regard, it will be interesting to observe whether specific childhood anxiety disorders (e.g., separation anxiety disorder, overanxious disorder) are associated with particular types of parental psychopathology (e.g., panic disorder, major depression, and so on).

Genetic Versus Environmental Transmission

Obviously, the studies reviewed above do not address the issue of mode of transmission, that is, environmental or genetic transmission. The top-down and bottom-up studies indicate that anxiety disorders tend to run in families, but only investigations utilizing methodologies common to genetic research (twin studies, adoption studies) can assess whether a hereditary component is present. What family studies can accomplish, in this regard, is to generate "negative proof," that is, if a higher frequency of a disorder is not observed among biological relatives, then genetic factors can not be involved.

In a review of genetic factors in the transmission of anxiety disorders, Torgersen (1988) concluded that panic disorder, phobic disorders, and obsessive-compulsive disorder seem to be influenced by genetic factors. In contrast, generalized anxiety disorder and posttraumatic stress disorder do not appear to be mediated through genetic transmission.

Two interesting questions emerge regarding the mode of transmission of childhood anxiety disorders. If transmission is genetic, what, specifically is inherited? Conversely, if transmission is environmental, how, specifically, is it accomplished?

From a hereditary perspective, individual differences in infants' temperaments (e.g., Thomas, Chess, Birch, Hertzig, & Korn, 1963, and Kagan, 1988) and/or in arousal level and habituation to stimuli (Johnson & Melamed, 1979) may be related to the acquisition of fear and anxiety disorders in childhood. This may be referred to as *anxiety proneness* or *vulnerability,* but either case denotes an inherited "disposition" toward developing anxiety disorders. This point is reviewed in greater detail further on.

Such an inherited disposition may interact adversely with certain environmental events, such as stressful life events (see below) or family interaction patterns and child-rearing practices. In this regard, the mother-child relationship repeatedly has been implicated, on both theoretical and empirical grounds, as an etiologic factor in the development of separation anxiety disorder and school phobia (e.g., Berg & McGuire, 1974; Eisenberg,1958; Hersov, 1960). Generally, mothers are described as overprotective, having separation anxiety issues of their own, and reinforcing dependency and lack of autonomy in their children.

The notion that maternal psychopathology plays a causal and/or maintenance role in children's anxiety disorders is of considerable importance since inferences have been drawn regarding intervention (Eisenberg, 1958). Considerably more research is needed regarding the relative roles (alone and in combination) of hereditary and family interaction variables.

STRESSFUL LIFE EVENTS

In a review of the adult literature, Monroe and Wade (1988) concluded that the available evidence suggests a relationship between life events and the development of anxiety disorders. Unfortunately, at least to our knowledge, almost no data exists pertaining to an association between life events and the onset of anxiety disorders in childhood.

From our clinical experience, it is clear that the onset and exacerbation of childhood anxiety disorders often are precipitated by stressful life occurrences. This particularly appears to be the case for separation anxiety disorder and school phobia, which may develop (or exacerbate) following a loss, such as illness or death of a significant other, or a move to a new neighborhood or school. In this regard, Gittelman-Klein and Klein (1980) reported that in their experience approximately 80% of school refusers show an onset associated with one of the aforementioned events.

Interestingly, early studies that were conducted following major traumatic events (e.g., cyclone, war zone, desegregation) have consistently shown negative results (Gordon, 1977; Martinez-Monfort & Dreger, 1972; Ziv & Israeli, 1973). A methodological problem common to each of these investigations, however, is exclusive reliance on children's self-ratings of their affective state. In contrast, more recent studies using more rigorous methodological approaches have shown adverse reactions in children exposed to massive traumas and natural disasters (Galante & Foa, 1986; Handford et al., 1986; Kinzie, Sack, Angell, Manson, & Rath, 1986; Malmquist, 1986; Terr, 1981).

Certainly there is a major difference between children who have a pattern of attachment disrupted and those who experience a major traumatic or life-threatening event. It may be that children who already are vulnerable or predisposed to developing anxiety disorders may be affected significantly by seemingly more innocuous events. In any event, significantly more research is needed on evaluating the association between life events and anxiety disorders in children before conclusions can be drawn.

DEVELOPMENTAL FACTORS

Clinical experience and existing empirical research indicate that certain fears are common to different developmental stages during infancy, childhood, and adolescence. Thus, the likelihood or risk of developing fears vary according to developmental level. This not only is of importance when examining risk; the developmental appropriateness of fear must be taken into account when distinguishing between normal fears and clinically significant anxiety disorders. In this regard, Miller, Barrett, and Hampe (1974) outlined diagnostic criteria for phobia that included the following criterion: "Is not age or stage specific" (p. 90). No such exclusionary criteria is included in DSM-III or DSM-III-R, which is used more commonly, at least in this country, for diagnosing psychiatric disorders (although the notion is implicit that normal variations of functioning should not be diagnosed).

Morris and Kratochwill (1983) have summarized the available data on normative fears in children from birth to 12 years of age (see Table 5.6). As indicated, considerable variability occurs in the nature of children's fears from year to year during the first 12 years of life.

Common fears in adolescence have been investigated by Croake and Knox (1971) in a sample of 212 ninth-grade students. Their findings are presented in Table 5.7.

The above data suggests that there are certain "at risk" periods for the development of specific fears during childhood and adolescence. In this sense, these fears can be considered "normal" or developmentally appropriate. However, if an age-appropriate fear is found to be excessive (i.e., over and beyond what would be expected in a normal child of that age) *and* cause impairment in functioning or high levels of subjective distress, a psychiatric diagnosis and intervention probably should be considered.

NEUROLOGICAL FACTORS

There is a long tradition, now pretty much abandoned, of dichotomizing psychiatric disorders between organic and functional disorders. Anxiety disorders are prime examples of conditions that would have

TABLE 5.6
Common Fears in Children

0 - 6 months:	Loss of support, loud noises
7 - 12 months:	Fear of strangers, fear of sudden, unexpected, and looming objects
1 year:	Separation from parent, toilet, injury, strangers
2 years:	A multitude of fears including loud noises (vacuum cleaners, sirens/alarms, trucks, and thunder), animals (e.g., large dogs), dark room, separation from parent, large objects/machines, change in personal environment
3 years:	Masks, dark, animals, separation from parent
4 years:	Parent separation, animals, dark, noises (including at night)
5 years:	Animals, "bad" people, dark, separation from parent, bodily harm
6 years:	Supernatural beings (e.g., ghosts, witches, "Darth Vader"), bodily injuries, thunder and lightning, dark, sleeping or staying alone, separation from parent
7 - 8 years:	Supernatural beings, dark, fears based on media events, staying alone, bodily injury
9 - 12 years:	Tests and examinations in school, school performance, bodily injury, physical appearance, thunder and lightning, death, dark (low percentage)

NOTE: Reprinted with permission from Morris, R. J., and Kratochwill, T. R., *Treating Childrens' Fears and Phobias*, © Copyright 1983, Pergamon Press PLC.

been considered functional syndromes. The expectation clearly has been that impaired brain function is not a factor in the origin of anxiety states. However, recent work by Shaffer and co-workers calls into question this popularly held notion. To investigate the long-term significance of neurological soft signs in children, Shaffer et al. (1985) evaluated adolescents who had been part of a population screening for neurological and cognitive status in childhood. The adolescents who had had soft signs in childhood were significantly more likely to have anxiety symptoms than those free of signs in childhood 28% (8/29) vs. 5% (3/57). As the authors state, "the presence of early soft signs was

TABLE 5.7

Common Fears in Adolescence

| | Sex | | |
Category	Male	Female	Total Sample
Animals	9.04%	10.55%	9.79%
Future	10.97	8.62	9.79
Supernatural phenomena	8.39	9.68	9.03
Natural phenomena	6.62	10.87	8.74
Personal appearance	8.47	9.17	8.82
Personal relations	10.56	10.56	10.56
School	10.37	10.05	10.21
Home	11.71	10.21	10.95
Safety	8.77	8.46	8.61
Political	13.02	12.35	12.68

NOTE: From "A second look at adolescent fears" by J. W. Croake and F. H. Knox, 1971, *Adolescence*, 6, 279-284. Adapted with permission.

associated with increased risk for a diagnosis of an anxiety-withdrawal disorder, especially in the presence of early anxiety" (p. 348).

Soft signs are believed to reflect nonlocalized brain dysfunctions that are not associated with gross anatomical abnormalities. However, it is thought that an association exists between childhood obsessive-compulsive disorder and specific, localized dysfunction of the nervous system. Several investigations now point in this direction (Behar et al., 1984; Wise & Rapoport, 1989). A single case of a clear cut anxiety syndrome in a boy with a brain tumor has been reported (Blackman & Wheler, 1987). The report by Cantwell & Baker (1987) that children with speech and language disorders were vulnerable to the development of anxiety symptoms is also consistent with a relationship between central nervous system dysfunction and anxiety disorders, at least in some instances.

It is likely that the previously held notions regarding the total dissociation between subtle brain dysfunction and anxiety symptoms is not tenable. Unfortunately, our understanding of soft signs is insufficient to permit the formulation of hypotheses regarding specific aspects of neurodevelopment that may be relevant to the regulation of anxiety in children.

DRUG REACTIONS

In adults, the possibility of triggering anxiety states with various compounds is well known. The ability of some drugs to induce specific anxiety states has obvious clinical implications for the proper diagnosis and treatment of patients with anxiety disorders; moreover, it may have heuristic implications for our understanding of the pathophysiology of anxiety (as for the panicogenic effect of cocaine in some adults). Although it is likely that drugs of abuse can induce severe fear reactions in some children and adolescents, full anxiety syndromes that continue after drug exposure have not been reported. Relevant to this issue, however, is the authors' experience treating several hundred children with hyperactivity. We have seen several instances of separation anxiety that coincided with the onset of stimulant treatment. In one child, the anxiety disorder occurred when the stimulant medication (dextroamphetamine) was withdrawn after several months of treatment. In addition, there is a report of a child with Tourette disorder in whom a school phobia occurred de novo each of three times he was treated with pimozide (a neuroleptic often used in Tourette disorder) (Linet, 1985).

TEMPERAMENT

It is now well-established that children differ from birth or shortly thereafter on a number of temperamental characteristics (Berger, 1985). It has been noted that a specific aspect of early temperament is likely to be one of the developmental precursors to anxiety disorders in children. In a series of elegant studies, Kagan and his colleagues have quantified aspects of social behavior in toddlers (Reznick, Kagan, & Snidman, 1986; Kagan, Reznick, & Snidman, 1987; Kagan, 1988). Not only have these investigators documented the presence of social inhibition in normal children, but they have shown also that this early temperamental characteristic, identified during the first 2 years of life, is relatively stable in a subgroup up to mid-childhood, that is, to age 7. The finding that this personality characteristic is stable is provocative since it might identify a set of interactional features that may affect later function. Could this be a premorbid feature of childhood anxiety disorders that predisposes to later anxious symptomatology? If so, are there influential environmental factors? Such relationships have been postulated. So far, no direct evidence exists. A small study of 2- to 7-year-old offspring of adults with panic disorder found them to have more social inhibition than children of normal adults; however, they were not significantly different from children of depressed adults (Rosenbaum et al., 1988). Unfortunately, the patient samples were too small to draw conclusions. The results are nevertheless encouraging, and the study of children of adults with anxiety disorders deserves further investigation.

SUMMARY

We have reviewed a variety of factors that may alone or in combination contribute to the development of anxiety disorders in children. Particularly striking is research that suggests that anxiety disorders aggregate within biological families, especially first-degree relatives. The potential causative roles of familial environment versus hereditary factors need to be explored more fully in future investigations.

The role of common but stressful life events in the genesis and maintenance of childhood anxiety disorders has been observed clinically but needs to be examined in controlled studies. Of particular interest is whether childhood anxiety disorders are more likely to be associated with specific types or categories of stressors (e.g., separation from attachment figures) than other forms of childhood psychopathology.

6

COURSE AND RELATIONSHIP TO ADULT PSYCHOPATHOLOGY

The focus of this chapter is on our knowledge of the long-term outcome of childhood and adolescent anxiety disorders and their link to adult psychopathology. The ultimate fate of ill children is important for an understanding of all forms of psychopathology. There is obvious concern about the eventual outcome for children whose adjustment is marred by anxiety that not only causes misery to the child and his or her family, but also impairs functioning by restricting the child's range of activities. We need to know if children who are in difficulty are likely to require care later on. Parents' concern is for the welfare of their children; community members want to project the need for treatment resources; professionals look to the development of treatments that can modify the later impairments of childhood psychopathology, if they occur.

Parents who have a school phobic child, whether due to separation or social anxiety, regularly wish to know if their child will go through life unable to enter new situations, resistant to tackle a job, and so on. Long-term studies are essential to provide a rational answer, but longitudinal clinical observations do more than inform about what can be expected over time: They provide important information about the nature of psychopathology. This issue is especially pertinent to children who, by virtue of the developmental process, inevitably undergo major psychological changes. Early anxiety might represent a temporary dysregulation (or a *phase,* a term some are fond of because it dismisses automatically the potential importance of the difficulties). Alternately, early anxiety might represent a stable pattern that remains unchanged, or it may put children at risk for other difficulties. Long-term follow-up studies can clarify these issues and help determine the relationship among disorders.

As discussed in Chapter 2, there is evidence that anxiety and depressive disorders frequently co-occur in the same individuals. Following-up children with either disorder may clarify the nature of this clinical relationship or comorbidity. For this purpose, the study of children offers major advantages over adults. The children offer the opportunity to observe the disorder before the complicating influences of chronicity of illness have taken place. If it is known that a childhood condition and an adult condition are associated, the search for specific etiologies can focus on the childhood form that has not been altered by complications due to chronicity or by previous treatment. In sum, knowledge of the relationship between early and later illness leads to an understanding of the development and nature of the adult disorder and may facilitate its study. The study of the adult fate of childhood anxiety has humane, practical, and theoretical implications.

The relationship between early and later anxiety disorders is receiving special attention because of findings from the largest psychiatric epidemiological study conducted (Robins et al., 1984). The National Institute of Mental Health (NIMH) Epidemiologic Catchment Area community survey from five U.S. geographical areas evaluated over 18,000 adults for lifetime prevalence of major DSM-III psychiatric disorders. First, anxiety disorders were reported by 14.6% of the respondents and were the most frequent disorders. In contrast, lifetime prevalence for major depressive disorder was 5.8%, for alcohol disorder it was 13.3% (Christie et al., 1988). Second, the median age of onset for anxiety disorders was 15; therefore, half the affected adults had their first symptoms before the age of 15. No other condition had such early onsets. For example, the median age of onset for major depression was 24 (Christie et al., 1988). These two confluent findings — a high rate of adult anxiety disorders and their origin in childhood — highlight the potential significance of childhood anxiety disorders.

SEPARATION ANXIETY DISORDER AND SCHOOL PHOBIA

Klein (1964) was the first to postulate a specific relationship between an adult and childhood anxiety disorder. He conjectured that severe separation anxiety in childhood seemed to be a precursor of adult panic disorder. This observation of the developmental pattern stemmed from childhood histories reported by adults with panic disorder. Klein (1964) noted that of 32 inpatients with agoraphobia and panic attacks, 50% had had severe separation anxiety in childhood with associated functional impairment such as school refusals, inability to attend summer camp, and so on. Moreover, such histories were not reported by other types of patients. Therefore, a specific link between pathological levels of separation anxiety during early development and a specific adult anxiety disorder was postulated. This hypothesis has important clinical implications. For one, it would argue for the distinctiveness of panic disorder from other adult anxiety disorders. Also, it might provide a means of refining the adult diagnosis that is undoubtedly heterogeneous, with multiple etiologies subsumed within it. Therefore, the review of the relationship between childhood and adult anxiety addresses an important contemporary theory of psychopathology and holds special developmental interest. It is noteworthy that the above hypothesis is not the only instance in which a specific childhood disturbance is said to lead to another specific adult disorder. Early asocial, "shut-in," schizoid adjustment has been linked to early onset schizophrenia, which has a chronic course (Gittelman-Klein, R., & Klein, 1969).

Three investigational strategies can be used to evaluate the relationship between childhood and adult anxiety: (1) The relationship between child and adult anxiety can be studied through the family study and history methods. The literature on this topic is reviewed in Chapter 5 and is not repeated here; (2) Longitudinal studies that follow-up anxious children over time, obviously, the longer the better; and (3) Retrospective or follow-back studies that examine the rate of anxiety in the childhood of adult patients with anxiety disorders. The last investigative method is inferior to the prospective follow-up of children since it is vulnerable to multiple sources of retrospective distortions. Some individuals may reframe their early life in terms of their current difficulties introducing inaccuracy in their recollection of childhood events, and others may have forgotten early symptomatology.

Most of the literature pertaining to the long-term outcome of childhood anxiety and its link to adult anxiety has been reviewed elsewhere (Gittelman, 1986; Gittelman & Klein, 1985); little new empirical information has appeared since, so that the information presented largely recapitulates the previous review.

LONGITUDINAL STUDIES

For the sake of providing a full picture of the nature of anxiety in children, we summarize the little there is of the literature on the stability of fears and anxiety in children from two types of studies: One group of studies has followed-up children drawn from the general population and the other has focused on children who were seen for treatment because of anxiety.

Follow-Up Studies of Anxious Children in the General Population

Several studies that have looked specifically at anxiety in normal children have reported that fears and shyness are relatively stable over time (Emde & Schmidt, 1978; MacFarlane, Allen, & Honzik, 1954; Richman, Stevenson, & Graham, 1982; Rutter, Tizard, & Whitmore, 1981). In England, Richman et al. (1982) obtained behavioral information from mothers of all 3 year olds in a specific geographical area. These same children were reevaluated five years later, at age 8. A number of children were judged to have developed a neurotic disorder at follow-up. (This class of psychopathology is generally believed to encompass anxiety and depressive disorders. Since depression is exceedingly rare in early childhood, it is most likely that the bulk of the neurotic children were predominantly anxious.) Richman found that the 8-year-old neurotic children already had an excess of anxiety at age 3. No feature of the child's adjustment at age 3 other than anxiety was associated with later neurosis. In addition and importantly, the negative impact of early anxiety was consistent: It was associated with later anxiety, but not with any other psychopathology, showing specificity in the course of anxiety in childhood. Therefore, if anxiety is relatively excessive in early development it seems to incur a risk for later anxiety, but not for other deviance. Early childhood anxiety in normal children appears to be a *specific* risk factor for later anxious symptomatology.

Rutter and associates obtained similar findings in the classical Isle of Wight epidemiologic study (Rutter, Tizard, & Whitmore, 1981). They conducted systematic clinical evaluations of a total population children at two time points, ages 11 and 15. As was the case in the Richman study, anxiety diagnoses were not used; instead, children with anxiety or depression were grouped into an emotional disorder category. The children who had an emotional disorder at age 11 were twice as likely than the rest of the group to have one at age 15. An important additional finding was that none of those with emotional disorders at 11 had developed a conduct disorder subsequently. Therefore, anxiety early on did not incur a risk for a variety of behavior problems. Instead, it predicted similar psychopathology.

In contrast to the above epidemiological studies, a U.S. questionnaire study did not find that ratings of anxiety showed stability of dysfunction in a population of children studied between 2 and 6 years of age, and reevaluated seven years later (Fischer, Rolf, Hasazi, & Cummings, 1984). However, unlike the previous British studies, this investigation relied on rating scales filled out by parents and did not undertake clinical assessments. As we noted in Chapter 3, there are no satisfactory parent scales for the identification and quantification of anxiety. It would be ill-advised to reach any conclusions based on such methodology, especially if it is inconsistent with results obtained from clinical evaluations.

As we noted in Chapter 5, social inhibition in children has been found to be a temperamental feature with significant consistency from toddlerhood (21 months) through mid-childhood (7 years). Although social inhibition is likely to be the result of anxious concern in children, it is not yet known whether it is associated with overt anxiety symptoms, and whether socially inhibited toddlers are at greater risk for anxiety disorders relative to other children.

In summary, studies of normal children (or nonpatients) indicate that, in the main, anxiety symptoms disappear with time; but there is a subgroup in whom they remain, and they cannot be dismissed as regularly ephemeral. Importantly, the results indicate that when the later functioning of anxious children is deleteriously affected, it is because the children continue to suffer from anxiety symptoms. Finally, early childhood anxiety does not appear to put children at risk for other types of behavioral or emotional difficulties.

Follow-Up Studies of Clinical Groups

None of the published longitudinal studies of anxiety in children identified in clinical settings has provided systematic diagnostic assessments of the children at the time they were identified or at follow-up. Consequently, this literature is summarized with reservations concerning the authors' ability to generalize from it to clinical childhood anxiety disorders as currently defined.

The most frequently studied children have been school phobic children. This patient group does not constitute a discrete diagnostic entity but is likely to have a large proportion of children with separation anxiety disorder (see Chapter 2).

Of the published studies, five have reported on the outcome of outpatient school phobic children and adolescents, five have dealt with hospitalized cases of school phobia, and one included both in- and outpatients. The studies are listed in Table 6.1. In addition, the results of an ongoing study whose results are unpublished are summarized (Klein & Mannuzza, unpublished data).

Inpatient Studies

The outcome of previously hospitalized school phobic children has been reported in a large series of carefully evaluated adolescents. Berg, Butler, and Hall (1976) found that many were experiencing adjustment difficulties 3 years after discharge, and that their condition was worse after 3 years than it had been 1 year after discharge. Half had impaired school attendance, between 50% and 70% had other symptomatology. Five (5%) had developed agoraphobia. Surprisingly, IQ was associated with quality of adjustment, with brighter youngsters having worse outcomes.

In a report of the posthospital adjustment of 14 school phobic children, Weiss and Burke (1970) indicate that only one could be considered free of serious neurotic or personality problems. Yet, the group's overall functioning was satisfactory.

Roberts (1975) obtained follow-up information on less than half of 131 youngsters hospitalized for school phobia, 5 to 18 years after discharge. All were judged to suffer from anxiety, but only 25% from separation anxiety. In this limited sample, over half the patients continued to have impaired school attendance, and half rated themselves as having poor adjustment. Age of onset was not predictive of eventual outcome.

Another questionnaire study of 54 hospitalized school phobic children (80% of the original group), followed-up at least 2 years after discharge, found that 22% reported having difficulty going out alone; in 6% it was severe. Other outcome measures, including those pertain-

TABLE 6.1
Follow-Up Studies of School Phobic Children

INPATIENTS

Author	N	Original N	Time (Years)	Method	Controls	Follow-up status
Warren (1965)	16	16	6	Interview	No	44% with phobic symptoms (unspecified)
Weiss & Burk (1970)	9	14	6	Interview	No	(1) Overall function OK (2) 93% with serious "neurosis"
Berg (1976)	100	125	3	Interview	No	(1) 50% poor school attendance (2) 50% other problems (3) 5% with agoraphobia (4) IQ inversly related to outcome
Roberts (1975)	56	131	5 - 18	Questionnaire	No	(1) 100% with significant anxiety (2) 25% with separation anxiety (3) Over 50% poor school attendance (4) Age of onset not predictive
Boreham (1983)	54	67	2 YRS. >	Questionnaire	No	(1) 22% some agoraphobia (2) 6% agoraphobia (3) No salient mood social problems

OUTPATIENTS

Author	N	Original N	Time (Years)	Method	Controls	Follow-up status
Rodriguez et. al (1959)	41	?	1 to 7	Telephone & mail	No	(1) 30% still not in school (2) 30% moderate-severe impairment (3) 3 schizophrenic (4) Better outcome in Ss below 11

Author	N	Original N	Time (Years)	Method	Controls	Follow-up status
Coolidge et. al (1964)	49	49	9	Open ended interview	No	(1) 60% with adjustment problems (2) 20% with serious problems
Hampe (1973)	62	67	2	Parent ratings	No	(1) 35% received subsequent treatment (2) Treatment failures received more subsequent treatment (3) 13% dropped out of school (4) Most children were rated less phobic
Waldron (1976)	42	35	10	Interview	Yes 18 "neurotics" 20 normals	(1) No difference between phobics and "neurotics" (2) *Patients vs. normals* A. More neurotics than controls B. Worse work and social adjustment
Baker & Wills (1979)	67	71	6	Questionnaire	No	(1) 20% never back in school (2) Work history OK (3) Treatment response not related to long-term outcome
MIXED IN/OUTPATIENTS						
Flakierska et. al (1988)	35	35	17	Public records	Yes: 35 school controls	(1) No difference in school completion (2) No difference in marriage rate (3) Significantly more former patients received outpatient treatment as adults (4) Former patients had significantly fewer children

ing to mood, friendship patterns, and school or work attendance, yielded low rates of disturbance (Boreham, 1983).

Baker and Wills (1979) examined the occupational status of 67 school phobic children 6 years after discharge from outpatient treatment. A sizable proportion (almost 20%) had never resumed school. However, 85% were working or attending school full time. The work and educational status of the group was slightly worse than in the general population of similar sex and age. School return during treatment did not portend a more favorable work outcome.

These outcome studies have focused on hospitalized cases, yet it is unusual for the clinical management of school phobic children to include inpatient care. Therefore, outpatient studies are more pertinent to an understanding of the outcome of the more typical clinical cases of school phobia.

Berg and Jackson (1985) summarized the 10-year outcome of adolescents treated as inpatients at the average age of 14. Of an initial cohort of 168 youngsters, only 55 could be reinterviewed at follow-up. Unfortunately, the study did not use a standardized interview and did not include controls. Therefore, only the data that relied on public records, which provides more complete coverage, is somewhat informative. The rate of subsequent treatment was high: 14% had been seen as outpatients for reasons other than school-related problems and 5% had been hospitalized in psychiatric centers. These rates compare very disfavorably with those from the general population. IQ predicted outcome positively. This finding is directly opposite to that reported by the same investigators in another report (Berg, Butler, & Hall, 1976). In addition, those who received treatment before age 14 had a more favorable outcome. However, in the absence of knowledge regarding age of onset, the inverse relationship between age of treatment and follow-up status has ambiguous meaning.

Outpatient Studies

The earliest study was of 41 school phobic children (Rodriguez, Rodriguez, & Eisenberg, 1959). The authors relied on telephone and mail responses from the family and school, conducted from 1 to 7 years following outpatient treatment. School attendance had resumed on a regular basis in 70% of the group. In this sample, children below the age of 11 had a better outcome than older children. Moderate to severe maladjustment was apparently present in 30% of the children, three cases being considered schizophrenic. The nature of the psychiatric features at follow-up is ambiguous, because of the lack of clinical evaluations and diagnostic standards.

In a 9-year follow-up, Coolidge, Brodie, & Feeney (1964) interviewed mothers and most of 49 school phobic children. Sixty percent were judged to have some problems in adjustment, 20% with serious difficulty ranging from character disorder to psychosis, in spite of renewed school attendance. Only a minority were judged free of any limitation at follow-up.

Another early study of the status of 67 neurotic youngsters 6 years after admission to an inpatient unit reports that, of the 16 cases admitted with school phobia, 9 (56%) were well at follow-up; the remaining 7 continued to be in difficulty due to phobic symptoms (whose nature is not specified) (Warren, 1965). No other information is provided. Of the whole neurotic group, a sizable proportion (32%) had further serious psychiatric illness. Half had required further treatment. Of those who had been ill during the follow-up interval, one-half had developed other disorders. The neurotic children had a more variable outcome than those with conduct disorders, who frequently retained the same behavior disorder when they failed to recover. As has been found in studies of fears in nonpatient groups, the outcome of the neurotic youngsters suggests that patterns of early and late psychopathology are relatively consistent. Unfortunately, this study suffers from marked diversity in clinical composition. The young patients had a broad mixture of neurotic psychopathology, such as obsessive-compulsive, anorectic, and phobic symptoms. Since this conditions are likely to have contrasting clinical courses, results observed from the combination of these diverse patients provides little useful information.

A mixed group of phobic children, many of whom were school phobic, were followed-up 2 years after their participation in a controlled treatment study. This treatment study (Miller, Barrett, Hampe, & Noble, 1972) is discussed in Chapter 4. Parents filled out questionnaires on their children's overall adjustment and the severity of their fears. A marked reduction in fear ratings was found. However, 60% of the youngsters had received treatment during the follow-up interval. Age was negatively associated with outcome; the younger children were rated less symptomatic on behavior rating scales, but not on those related to anxiety.

The prospective study by Waldron (1976) compared 24 children who had had a school phobia with 18 neurotic children, and with a small group of carefully selected normal controls. At follow-up, no difference was found between the school phobic and neurotic children. Both patient groups had more frequent diagnoses of neurosis and personality disorders than controls. Also, they were felt to have worse occupational and interpersonal adjustments. Curiously, none of the controls received a psychiatric diagnosis. This negative finding highlights the necessity of using relatively large control groups so that the expected population rate of psychiatric disorder is detected. Studies using small groups of normals may under- or overestimate the prevalence of emotional disorders.

Flakierska, Lindstrom, and Gillberg (1988) surveyed public records of a complete cohort of 35 school phobic children first identified between 7 and 12 years of age, 15 to 20 years later, as well as a matched control group selected from health school records was identified. School and health and demographic history were the major outcomes. The school phobic children and controls did not differ in rate of school completion, in contact with social authorities, and in police contacts. Only the frequency of outpatient (but not inpatient) psychiatric treatment differentiated the adjustment of the two groups, with the school phobic group having had more treatment (31% vs. 11%). Diagnoses of neurotic depression and separation anxiety disorder were salient in the school phobic group, but their rate is not indicated.

A hyperventilation syndrome in children may be a variant of an anxiety syndrome whose chief symptom consists of episodes of overbreathing. Such children are likely to be treated primarily in pediatric services. Thirty children (ages 6 - 18) diagnosed in a medical clinic as having hyperventilation syndrome were followed-up by mail 2 to 28 years later (Herman, Stickler, & Lucas, 1981). Anxiety symptoms and hyperventilation were present in a large proportion of the group, suggesting that the syndrome may be a childhood anxiety disorder. At the same time, hyperventilation episodes might be only one symptom of an anxiety syndrome such as social phobia or separation anxiety disorder. Not enough is known about hyperventilation in children to settle the issue.

The follow-up studies presented have all consisted of clinical cases. Since these are likely to represent relatively severe or chronic cases, they do not provide information about the outcome of school phobic children in the general population. Only one investigation was found dealing with the outcome of school phobic children in a total school population (Ono, 1972). In this Japanese group, 1 year after the identification of 95 school phobic children, half were frequently absent from school. The short-term follow-up of this study limits its usefulness in predicting outcome; nevertheless, it suggests that continued difficulties in school attendance are not exceptional, at least in the short run, and that this outcome is not limited to clinical groups.

Klein and Mannuzza (unpublished data) are currently following-up a group of children who were treated for school phobia in the late 1960s (the treatment study has been summarized in Gittelman-Klein & Klein, 1971; 1980). Originally, the children were between 6 and 15 years of age. Almost all (42 of 45) had clinically significant separation anxiety in childhood but no diagnostic criteria were applied. The ones who did not respond to an intense behavioral intervention within 2 weeks were entered in a double-blind placebo controlled study of imipramine (a compound now established as an effective antidepressant and anti-panic agent in adults). At the time of this reporting, 54 former patients and 60 community identified controls have been followed-up. Each was interviewed without knowledge of previous history, using a semi-structured interview that provides DSM-III and DSM-III-R disorders of adulthood as well as the childhood disorders of separation anxiety disorder, attention deficit hyperactivity disorder, and conduct disorder (The CHAMPS [Mannuzza & Klein, 1987]). When reevaluated, the probands were 28 years of age on average (from 24 to 33 years), and the interval between the childhood referral and follow-up was close to 20 years.

Unexpectedly, the rate of major depression did not differ significantly between the probands and controls, although there were more depressive disorders among the probands than controls (31% vs. 18%). Neither did the two groups differ significantly in overall rate of anxiety disorders. However, there was a significantly greater rate of agoraphobia with panic disorder in the adults who had had separation anxiety in childhood than in controls, 7% vs. 0% (p. = .05). Social phobia was twice as prevalent in the probands than controls, but this difference was not significantly different.

These preliminary results, although not strong, are consistent with the hypothesis that early separation anxiety predisposes to panic disorder in later life. It is conceivable that treatment in childhood has some mitigating effect on prognosis, but such a relationship has not yet been examined.

This study has the major advantages of having a well-defined group of children whose evaluation in adulthood was done blindly applying uniform diagnostic criteria. Such studies are critical to a full understanding of the specific risks of early separation anxiety disorder for later adjustment. However, they are very difficult to do because large groups of well-defined anxious children are rare, and when they do exist they are very difficult to locate and reevalute.

OBSESSIVE-COMPULSIVE DISORDER

Obsessive-compulsive disorder is the only other childhood anxiety disorder in which course has been studied. Consistently, it has been reported that the onset of adult obsessive-compulsive disorder is in early life, in the early 20s on the average. This finding indicates that in many cases, the disorder is chronic from adolescence on. However, these findings do not indicate the frequency of stability over time.

Swedo and Rapoport (1989) report that in most adolescents the onset begins with a single obsession or compulsion that may last several years until more elaborate rituals gradually set in. From retrospective histories obtained from children and adolescents, the disorder appears to be fluctuating, usually with gradual shifts in severity.

In a 2- to 7-year follow-up (mean 4 years) of patients evaluated at the NIMH, almost 70% still retained the original disorder at follow-up, but 30% were free of any psychiatric illness. The rate of overall pathology at follow-up was strikingly more elevated in the obsessive-compulsive adolescents than in controls (Flament, Koby, et al., in press; Swedo & Rapoport, 1989). In addition to the longitudinal study of this clinical group, Rapoport and colleagues conducted a two-year prospective evaluation of adolescents with obsessive-compulsive disorder identified in an epidemiological survey. The rate of obsessive-compulsive disorder in those with early obsessive-compulsive disorder far exceeded the rate in controls (46% vs. 14%). Moreover, whereas 76% of the controls had no diagnosis at follow-up, only 15% of the adolescents with previous OCD were free of a psychiatric diagnosis. The stability of the disorder may be associated with severity since the prevalence of OCD at follow-up was so much higher in the clinical group than in the community sample. However, the two investigations are not completely equivalent since the clinical sample was followed-up for 4 years and the epidemiological group for only 2 years. Nevertheless, it is suggestive of a relationship between severity and chronicity.

FOLLOW-BACK STUDIES

As we stated earlier, if anxiety disorders put children at risk for anxiety disorders in adulthood, the childhood histories of adult patients with anxiety disorders should have a disproportionate rate of anxiety disorders compared with adults free of anxiety disorders. The following studies have addressed this issue.

Abe (1972) studied a general population of relatively young women by approaching mothers who were bringing their 3-year-old children to a public health clinic for routine check-ups in Japan. Two findings emerged: (1) There was a strong association in the women's self-reports of anxiety symptoms in adulthood and childhood, and (2) anxiety symptoms regularly began in childhood or adolescence; none had arisen during the adulthood of this group of women. There were no diagnostic refinements and the types of early and later anxiety are unclear.

There have been several investigations of early separation anxiety in outpatient adults with agoraphobia/panic disorder. Berg, Marks, McGuire, and Lipsedge (1974) examined the frequency of previous school phobia self-reports from a questionnaire obtained from the English nationwide samples of nearly 800 agoraphobic women, and compared them to a group of 57 neurotics treated in an outpatient clinic. Both patient groups reported a very high frequency of school phobia (22%). The authors concluded that childhood school phobia is a precursor of later neurotic illness, but not of agoraphobia specifically. This report would have benefited from a more detailed description of the neurotic group. For example, it is not stated whether the presence of panic or agoraphobia was ruled out in the neurotic group.

Klein and his associates (Klein, Zitrin, Woerner, & Ross, 1983; Zitrin, Klein, Woerner, & Ross, 1983) conducted treatment studies of imipramine and behavioral treatment in outpatient agoraphobic and simple phobic patients. At intake, the patients were interviewed concerning the presence of clinically significant separation anxiety in childhood and adolescence. Summaries of these interviews done during the diagnostic process were reviewed and each patient was rated for the presence of separation anxiety by a senior psychologist. Assessments of childhood and adolescent separation anxiety were available for 66 of 77 agoraphobic and 66 of 81 simple phobic patients.

In some cases, separation anxiety could not be ascertained because family members had been unusually closeknit and usual separations had not taken place regularly except for work or school. In such families, children never went to camp, children and parents socialized with the immediate family circle, the child never stayed at friends' homes or went anywhere without the parents. This familial pattern is suggestive of tight attachment bonds or of avoidance of separation among the family members.

In childhood as well as adolescence, agoraphobic patients had reported more separation anxiety than patients with simple phobia (separation anxiety in childhood: 14% vs. 24%; adolescence: 15% vs. 4%). However, when the two genders were examined separately, the difference in separation anxiety seemed true of female but not male agoraphobic patients (48% vs. 15%, respectively). Thus, a history of separation anxiety disorder did not appear to be related to agoraphobia in the men, only in the women. In addition, Gittelman & Klein (1985) found that not only was the rate of separation anxiety greater in agoraphobic women than in simple phobic patients but, during adolescence, a significantly larger proportion (43.5% vs. 14%) had not separated from their families.

Two studies conducted in Italy have reviewed a history of school phobia and anxiety in adult patients with panic disorder. The adults with panic plus avoidance or agoraphobia differed from those with panic disorder without phobic avoidance. School phobia in childhood was reported to have occurred much more often in the 25 adults suffering from panic with agoraphobia (60%) compared to the 14 patients who had no avoidance associated with their panic disorder (0%) (Deltito, Perugi, Maremmani, Mignani, & Cassano, 1986).

The second study of 264 adults with panic disorder from the same group of investigators did not replicate these findings. As others have observed, the authors reported that patients with a history of childhood separation anxiety had an earlier onset than those without the childhood disorder (Perugi et al., 1988). However, these studies did not confirm that childhood separation anxiety was more typical of women than men with panic/agoraphobia disorder as had been reported by Gittelman & Klein (1985).

SUMMARY

The outcome studies published so far do not provide a clear picture of the psychiatric sequelae of childhood and adolescent anxiety disorders except for recent investigations of children with obsessive-compulsive disorder. Several investigators report a high rate of neurotic disturbance in the subsequent adjustment of school phobic children. However, the nature of the emotional impairment is unclear. The single study of the later work history of school phobic children does not indicate the likelihood of occupational handicaps in most cases (Baker & Wills, 1979). No predictors of outcome have been identified. Early age of onset has not been a consistent predictor of good outcome. Successful short-term clinical management has also failed to portend a better long-term status.

A longitudinal study of children with separation anxiety that has not yet been published found an excess of panic disorder and a trend for an increase in depressive disorder and social phobic disorder in the formerly anxious children compared with controls. Obsessive-compulsive disorder has been found to be relatively stable in previously treated children and in community cases as well.

The relationship between child and adult anxiety disorders has been examined also by assessing the childhood histories of adult patients. Anxious adults report more anxiety in childhood than controls. However, the notion that this is true of only one type of adult anxiety disorder, or that adult agoraphobia and panic disorder are specifically associated with separation anxiety disorder in childhood has not been documented consistently.

There is clear continuity of anxiety symptomatology through human development, but it remains unclear whether there are specific relationships between childhood and adult forms of anxiety. The evidence on this point is still inconclusive.

REFERENCES

Abe, K. (1972) Phobias and nervous symptoms in childhood and maturity: Persistence and associations. *British Journal of Psychiatry, 120*, 275-283.

Achenbach, T. M. (1978). The child behavior profile: 1. Boys aged 6-11. *Journal of Consulting and Clinical Psychology, 46*, 478-488.

Achenbach, T. M., & Edelbrock, C. S. (1979). The child behavior profile: 2. Boys aged 12-16 and girls aged 6-11 and 12-16. *Journal of Consulting and Clinical Psychology, 47*, 223-233.

Adams, P. L. (1973). *Obsessive children*. New York: Penguin.

Ainsworth, M. (1978). *Patterns of Attachment*. Hillsdale, NJ: Erlbaum.

American Psychiatric Association (1962). *Diagnostic and statistical manual of mental disorders* (2nd ed.). Washington, DC: Author.

American Psychiatric Association (1980). *Diagnostic and statistical manual of mental disorders* (3rd ed.). Washington, DC: Author.

American Psychiatric Association (1987). *Diagnostic and statistical manual of mental disorders* (3rd ed.-revised). Washington, DC: Author.

Anderson, J. C., Williams, S., McGee, R., & Silva, P. A. (1987). DSM-III disorders in preadolescent children. *Archives of General Psychiatry, 44*, 69-76.

Ayllon, T., Smith, D., & Rogers, M. (1970). Behavioral management of school phobia. *Journal of Behavioral Therapy and Experimental Psychiatry, 1*, 125-130.

Baker, H., & Wills, U. (1978). School phobia: Classification and treatment. *British Journal of Psychiatry, 132*, 492-499.

Baker, H., & Wills, U. (1979). School phobic children at work. *British Journal of Psychiatry, 135*, 561-564.

Ballenger, J. C., Burrows, G. D., DuPont, R. L., Lesser, I. M., Noyes, R., Pecknold, J. C., Rifkin, A., & Swinson, R. P. (1988). Alprazolam in panic disorder and agoraphobia: Results from a multicenter trial. *Archives of General Psychiatry, 45*, 412-422.

Barnes, G. G. (1985). Systems theory and family theory. In M. Rutter & L. Hersov (Eds.), *Child and adolescent psychiatry: Modern approaches* (2nd ed.), pp. 216-229. Oxford: Blackwell Scientific.

Barrios, B. A., Hartmann, D. P., & Shigetomi, C. (1981). Fears and anxieties in children. In E. J. Mash & L. G. Terdal (Eds.), *Behavioral assessment of childhood disorders* (pp. 259-304). New York: Guilford.

Behar, D., Rapoport, J. L., Berg, C. J., Denckla, M. B., Mann, L., Cox, C.,Fedio, P., Zahn, T., & Wolfman, M. G. (1984). Computerized tomography and neuropsychological test measures in adolescents with obsessive-compulsive disorder. *American Journal of Psychiatry, 141*, 363-369.

Beidel, D. C., & Turner, S. M. (1988). Comorbidity of test anxiety and other anxiety disorders in children. *Journal of Abnormal Child Psychology, 16*, 275-287.

Berg, I. (1976). School phobia in children of agoraphobic women. *British Journal of Psychiatry, 128*, 86-89.

Berg, I., Butler, A., & Hall, G. (1976). The outcome of adolescent school phobia. *British Journal of Psychiatry, 128*, 80-85.

Berg, I., Butler, A., & Pritchard, J. (1974). Psychiatric illness in the mothers of school phobic adolescents. *British Journal of Psychiatry, 125*, 466-467.

Berg, I., & Jackson, A. (1985). Teenage school refusers grow up: A follow-up study of 168 subjects, ten years on average after in-patient treatment. *British Journal of Psychiatry, 47*, 366-370.

Berg, I., Marks, I., McGuire, R., & Lipsedge, M. (1974). School phobia and agoraphobia. *Psychological Medicine, 4*, 428-434.

Berg, I., & McGuire, R. (1974). Are mothers of school-phobic adolescents overprotective? *British Journal of Psychiatry, 124*, 10-13.

Berg, C. J., Rapoport, J. L., & Flament, M. (1985). The Leyton Obsessional Inventory — Child Version. *Psychopharmacology Bulletin, 21*, 1057-1059.

Berger, M. (1985). Temperament and individual differences. In M. Rutter & L. Hersov (Eds.), *Child and adolescent psychiatry: Modern approaches* (pp. 3-16). Oxford: Blackwell Scientific.

Berney, T., Kolvin, I., Bhate, S. R., Garside, R. F., Jeans, J., Kay, B., & Scarth, L. (1981). School phobia: A therapeutic trial with clomipramine and short-term outcome. *British Journal of Psychiatry, 138*, 110-118.

Bernstein, G. A., & Garfinkel, B. D. (1986). School phobia: The overlap of affective and anxiety disorders. *Journal of the American Academy of Child Psychiatry, 25*, 235-241.

Bernstein, G. A., & Garfinkel, B. D. (1988). Pedigrees, functioning, and psychopathology in families of school phobic children. *American Journal of Psychiatry, 145*, 70-74.

Bernstein, G. A., Garfinkel, B. D., & Borchardt, C. M. (1987, October). *Imipramine versus alprazolam for school phobia.* Paper presented at the annual meeting of the American Academy of Child and Adolescent Psychiatry, Washington, DC.

Blackman, M., & Wheler, G. H. T. (1987). A case of mistaken identity: A fourth ventricular tumor presenting as school phobia in a 12 year boy. *Canadian Journal of Psychiatry, 32*, 584-587.

Blagg, N. R., & Yule, W. (1984). The behavioral treatment of school refusal — comparative study. *Behavior Research and Therapy, 22*, 119-127.

Bolton, D., Collins, S., & Steinberg, D. (1983). The treatment of obsessive-compulsive disorder in adolescence: A report of fifteen cases. *British Journal of Psychiatry, 142*, 456-464.

Boreham, J. (1983). A follow-up study of 54 persistent school refusers. *Association for Child Psychology and Psychiatry News, 15*, 8-14.

Bowlby, J. (1969). *Attachment and loss, Vol. 1: Attachment.* New York: Basic Books.

Bowlby, J. (1973). *Attachment and loss, Vol. 2: Separation anxiety and anger.* New York: Basic Books.

Brenner, C. (1974). *An elementary textbook for psychoanalysis.* New York: Anchor.

Buglass, D., Clarke, J., Henderson, A. S., Kreitman, N., & Presley, A. S. (1977). Study of agoraphobic housewives. *Psychological Medicine, 7*, 73-86.

Cantwell, D. P., & Baker, L. (1987). The prevalence of anxiety disorders in children with communication disorders. *Journal of Anxiety Disorders, 1*, 239-248.

Castaneda, A., McCandless, B., & Palermo, D. (1956). The children's form of the Manifest Anxiety Scale. *Child Development, 27*, 317-326.

Cattell, R. B., & Cattell, M. D. (1979). *The high school personality questionnaire.* Champaign, IL: The Institute for Personality and Ability Testing.

Cattell, R. B., & Coan, R. W. (1979). *The early school personality questionnaire.* Champaign, IL: The Institute for Personality and Ability Testing.

Cattell, R. B., Krug, S. E., & Scheier, I. H. (1976). *IPAT Anxiety Scale.* Champaign, IL: The Institute for Personality and Ability Testing.

Chambers, W. J., Puig-Antich, J., Hirsch, M., Paez, P., Ambrosini, P. J., Tabrizi, M. A., & Davies, M. (1985). The assessment of affective disorders in children and adolescents by semi-structured interview. *Archives of General Psychiatry, 42,* 696-702.

Christie, K. A., Burke, J. D., Regier, D. A., Rae, D. S., Boyd, J. H., & Locke, B. Z. (1988). Epidemiologic evidence for early onset of mental disorders and higher risk of drug abuse in young adults. *American Journal of Psychiatry, 145,* 971-975.

Clark, W. W., Tiegs, E. W., & Thorpe, L. P. (1953). *California Test of Personality Intermediate Form AA.* Monterey, CA: McGraw-Hill.

Coolidge, J. C., Brodie, R. D., & Feeney, B. (1964). A ten-year follow-up study of sixty-six school children. *American Journal of Orthopsychiatry, 34,* 675-684.

Costello, A. J., Edelbrock, C. S., Kessler, M., Kalas, R., & Klaric, S. A. (1983). *Diagnostic interview schedule for children.*

Croake, J. W., & Knox, F. H. (1971). A second look at adolescent fears. *Adolescence, 6,* 279-284.

Darwin, C. (1959). *On the origin of species by means of natural selection.* London: Murray.

Darwin, C. (1965). *The expression of emotions in man and animals.* Chicago: University of Chicago Press.

Deltito, J. A., Perugi, G., Maremmani, I., Mignani, V., Cassano, G. B. (1986). The importance of separation anxiety in the differentiation of panic disorder from agoraphobia. *Psychiatric Developments, 3,* 227-236.

Eisenberg, L. (1958). A study in the communication of anxiety. *American Journal of Psychiatry, 114,* 712-718.

Emde, R. F., & Schmidt, D. (1978). The stability of children's fears. *Child Development, 49,* 1277-1279.

Erikson, E. (1950). *Childhood and society.* New York: Norton.

Eysenck, H. J. (1967). *The biological basis of personality.* Springfield, IL: Charles C Thomas.

Eysenck, H. J., & Eysenck, S. B. G. (1975). *Eysenck Personality Questionnaire (Junior).* San Diego, CA: Educational and Industrial Testing Service.

Finch, A. J., Kendall, P. C., & Montgomery, L. E. (1974). Multidimensionality of anxiety in children: Factor structure of the Children's Manifest Anxiety Scale. *Journal of Abnormal Child Psychology, 2,* 331-336.

Fischer, M., Rolf, J. E., Hasazi, J. E., & Cummings, L. (1984). Follow-up of a preschool epidemiological sample: Cross-age continuities and predictions of later adjustment with internalizing and externalizing dimensions of behavior. *Child Development, 55,* 137-150.

Flakierska, N., Lindstrom, M., & Gillberg, C. (1988). School refusal: A 15-20 year follow-up study of 35 Swedish urban children. *British Journal of Psychiatry, 152,* 834-837.

Flament, M. F., Koby, E., Rapoport, J. L., Berg, C. J., Zahn, T., Cox, C., Denckla, M., & Lenane, M. (in press). Childhood obsessive compulsive disorder: A prospective follow-up study. *Journal of Child Psychology and Psychiatry.*

Flament, M. F., Rapoport, J. L., Murphy, D. L., Berg, C. J., & Lake, R. (1987). Biochemical changes during clomipramine treatment of childhood obsessive-compulsive disorder. *Archives of General Psychiatry, 44,* 219-225.

Flament, M., Rapoport, J. L., Murphy, D., Linnoila, M., Karoum, F., Potter, W., & Ismond, D. (1985). Clomipramine treatment of children with obsessive compulsive disorder: A double-blind controlled trial. *Archives of General Psychiatry, 42,* 977-986.

Francis, G. (1988). Childhood obsessive-compulsive disorder: Extinction of compulsive reassurance-seeking. *Journal of Anxiety Disorders, 2,* 361-366.

Francis, G., Last, C. G., & Strauss, C. C. (1988). [Avoidant disorder of children or adolescence]. Unpublished raw data.

Freud, A. (1965). *Normality and pathology in childhood: Assessments of development.* New York: International Universities Press.

Freud, S. (1894). *Draft E. How anxiety originates.* London: Hogarth.

Freud, S. (1917). *Introductory lectures on psychoanalysis, Lecture XXV.* London: Hogarth.

Freud, S. (1948). *Inhibitions, symptoms and anxiety.* London: Hogarth.

Freud, S. (1950). Analysis of a phobia in a five-year-old boy. In Freud, S., *Collected papers, Vol. 3.* London: Hogarth.

Galante, R., & Foa, D. (1986). An epidemiological study of psychic trauma and treatment effectiveness for children after a natural disaster. *Journal of the American Academy of Child Psychiatry, 25,* 357-363.

Gittelman, R. (1980). The role of psychological tests for differential diagnosis in child psychiatry. *Journal of the American Academy of Child Psychiatry, 19,* 413-438.

Gittelman, R. (1986). Childhood anxiety disorders: Correlates and outcomes. In R. Gittelman (Ed.), *Anxiety disorders of childhood.* New York: Guilford.

Gittelman, R., & Klein, D. F. (1985). Childhood separation anxiety and adult agoraphobia. In A. H. Tuma & J. D. Maser (Eds.). *Anxiety and the anxiety disorders* (pp. 389-402). Hillsdale, NJ: Laurence Erlbaum.

Gittelman-Klein, R., & Klein, D. F. (1973). School phobia: Diagnostic considerations in the light of impramine effects. *Journal of Nervous and Mental Disease, 156,* 199-215.

Gittelman-Klein, R. (1975). Psychiatric characteristics of the relatives of school phobic children. In D. V. S. Sankar (Ed.), *Mental health in children — Volume 1.* New York: PJD.

Gittelman-Klein, R. (1978). Validity of projective tests for psychodiagnosis in children. In R. L. Spitzer & D. F. Klein (Eds.), *Critical issues in psychiatric diagnosis* (pp. 141-166). New York: Raven.

Gittelman-Klein, R., & Klein, D. F. (1969). Premorbid asocial adjustment and prognosis in schizophrenia. *Journal of Psychiatric Research, 7,* 35-53.

Gittelman-Klein, R., & Klein, D. F. (1971). Controlled imipramine treatment of school phobia. *Archives of General Psychiatry, 25,* 204-207.

Gittelman-Klein, R., & Klein, D. F. (1980). Separation anxiety in school refusal and its treatment with drugs. In L. Hersov & I. Berg (Eds.), *Out of school* (pp. 321-341). New York: John Wiley.

Gordon, M. (1977). Cyclone Tracey II: The effects on Darwin. *Australian Psychologist, 12,* 55-82.

Goyette, C. H., Conners, C. K., & Ulrich, R. F. (1978). Normative data on the revised Conners parent and teacher ratings scales. *Journal of Abnormal Child Psychology, 6,* 221-236.

Graham, P., & Rutter, M. (1968). The reliability and validity of the psychiatric assessment of the child. II. Interview with the parents. *British Journal of Psychiatry, 114,* 581-592.

Gray, J. A. (1988). The neuropsychological basis of anxiety. In C. Last & M. Hersen (Eds.), *Handbook of anxiety disorders.* New York: Pergamon.

Hallam, R. S. (1974). Extinction of ruminations: A case study. *Behavior Therapy, 5,* 565-568.

Handford, H. A., Mayes, S. D., Mattison, R. E., Humphrey, F. J., Bagnato, S., Bixler, E. O., & Kales, J. D. (1986). Child and parent reaction to the Three Mile Island nuclear accident. *Journal of the American Academy of Child Psychiatry, 25,* 346-356.

Harlow, H. F., & Harlow, M. K. (1965). The affectional systems. In A. Schrier et al. (Eds.), *Behavior of nonhuman primates. Volume 2.* New York: Academic Press.

Harlow, H. F., & Harlow, M. K. (1971). Psychopathology in monkeys. In H. D. Kimmel (Ed.), *Experimental psychopathology.* New York: Academic Press.

Harlow, H. F., & Suomi, S. J. (1974). Induced depression in monkeys. *Behavioral Biology, 12,* 273-296.

Harms, E. (1967). *Origins of modern psychiatry* (pp. 168-181). Springfield, IL: Charles C Thomas.

Hathaway, S. R., & McKinley, J. C. (1951). *The Minnesota multiphasic personality inventory manual, (rev. ed.).* New York: The Psychological Corporation.

Herman, S. P., Stickler, G. B., & Lucas, A. R. (1981). Hyperventilation syndrome in children and adolescents: Long-term follow-up. *Pediatrics, 67,* 183-187.

Hersen, M. (1970). Behavior modification approach to a school phobia case. *Journal of clinical Psychology, 26,* 128-132.

Hershberg, S. G., Carlson, G. A., Cantwell, D. P., & Strober, M. (1982). Anxiety and depressive disorders in psychiatrically disturbed children. *Journal of clinical Psychiatry, 43,* 358-361.

Hersov, L. A. (1960). Persistent non-attendance at school. *Journal of Child Psychology and Psychiatry, 1,* 130-136.

Hoehn-Saric, E., Maisami, M., & Wiegand, D. (1987). Measurement of anxiety in children and adolescents using semistructured interviews. *Journal of the American Academy of Child and Adolescent Psychiatry, 26,* 541-545.

Hollingsworth, C., Tanguey, P., Grossman, L., & Pabst, P. (1980). Long-term outcome of obsessive compulsive disorder in childhood. *Journal of the American Academy of Child Psychiatry, 19,* 134-144.

Horney, K. (1945). *Our inner conflicts.* New York: W. W. Norton.

Izard, C. E. (1982). *Measuring emotions in infants and children* (pp. 3-18). Cambridge: Cambridge University Press.

Johnson, S. B., & Melamed, B. G. (1979). Assessment and treatment of children's fears. In B. B. Lahey & A. E. Kazdin (Eds.), *Advances in clinical child psychology. Volume 2.* New York: Plenum.

Jones, M. (1924). A laboratory study of fear. *Pedagogical Seminars, 31,* 308-315.

Judd, L. (1965). Obsessive compulsive neurosis in children. *Archives of General Psychiatry, 12,* 136-143.

Kagan, J. (1988). Biological bases of childhood shyness. *Science, 240,* 167-171.

Kagan, J., Reznick, J. S., & Snidman, N. (1987). The physiology and psychology of behavioral inhibition in young children. *Child Development, 58,* 1459-1473.

Kanner, L. (1959). The twenty-third Maudsley lecture: Trends in child psychiatry. *Journal of Mental Science, 105,* 581-593.

Kanner, L. (1961). American contributions to the development of child psychiatry. *Psychiatric Quarterly* (supplement), *35*, 1-12.

Kashani, J., McGee, R., Clarkson, S., Anderson, J., Walton, L., Williams, S., Silva, P., Robins, A., Cytryn, M., & McKnew, D. (1983). Depression in a sample of 9-year-old children: Prevalence and associated characteristics. *Archives of General Psychiatry, 40,* 1217-1223.

Keller, B. B. (1989). Cognitive assessment of obsessive-compulsive children. In J. L. Rapoport (Ed.), *Obsessive compulsive disorder* (pp. 33-40). New York: Associated Press.

Kennedy, W. A. (1965). School phobic: Rapid treatment of fifty cases. *Journal of Abnormal Psychology, 70,* 285-289.

Kierkegaard, S. (1944). *The concept of dread.* (W. Lownie, Trans.). Princeton, NJ: Princeton University Press. (Original work published 1844).

Kinzie, J. D., Sack, W. H., Angell, R. H., Manson, S., & Rath, B. (1986). The psychiatric effects of massive trauma on Cambodian children: I. The children. *Journal of the American Academy of Child Psychiatry, 25,* 370-376.

Klein, D. F. (1964). Delineation of two drug-responsive anxiety syndromes. *Psychopharmacologia, 3,* 397-408.

Klein, D. F. (1980). Anxiety reconceptualized. In D. F. Klein & J. G. Rabkin (Eds.), *Anxiety: New research and changing concepts* (pp. 235-262). New York: Raven Press.

Klein, R. (1989). [Imipramine treatment of childhood separation anxiety disorder]. Unpublished raw data (a).

Klein, R. (1989). [Clinical trial with alprazolam in separation anxiety disorder]. Unpublished raw data (b).

Klein, R. G. (in press). Treatment of anxiety in children. In N. Sartorius (Ed.), *Anxiety: Psychobiological and clinical perspectives.* Geneva: World Health Organization.

Klein, R. G., & Mannuzza, S. (1989). [Adult outcome of childhood separation anxiety disorder]. Unpublished raw data.

Klein, D. F., Zitrin, C. M., Woerner, M. G., & Ross, D. D. (1983). Treatment of phobias: II. Behavior therapy and supportive psychotherapy: Are there any specific and supportive ingredients? *Archives of General Psychiatry, 40,* 139-145.

Kolvin, I., Berney, T. P., & Bhate, S. R. (1984). Classification and diagnosis of depression in school phobia. *British Journal of Psychiatry, 145,* 347-357.

Kotsopoulos, S., & Mellor, C. (1986). Extralinguistic speech characteristics of children with conduct and anxiety disorders. *Journal of Child Psychology and Psychiatry, 27,* 99-108.

Kovacs, M. (1983a). The Children's Depression Inventory: A self-rated depression scale for school-aged youngsters. Pittsburgh, PA: University of Pittsburgh School of Medicine. Unpublished manuscript.

Kovacs, M. (1983b). The Interview Schedule for Children (ISC): Interrater and parent-child agreement. Pittsburgh, PA: University of Pittsburgh School of Medicine. Unpublished manuscript.

Lachar, D. (1982). *Personality inventory for children (PIC) revised format manual supplement.* Los Angeles: Western Psychological Services.

Landis, C. (1924). Studies of emotional reaction. *Journal of Comparative Psychology, 4,* 447-509.

Last, C. G. (1986). Modification of the K-SADS-P. Unpublished manuscript.

Last, C. G. (1987). Developmental considerations. In C. G. Last & M. Hersen (Eds.), *Issues in diagnostic research.* New York: Plenum.

Last, C. G., & Francis, G. (1988). School phobia. In B. Lahey & A. Kazdin (Eds.), *Advances in clinical child psychology: Volume 11*. New York: Plenum.

Last, C. G., Francis, G., Hersen, M., Kazdin, A. E., & Strauss, C. C. (1987). Separation anxiety and school phobia: A comparison using DSM-III criteria. *American Journal of Psychiatry, 144*, 653-657.

Last, C. G., Francis, G., & Strauss, C.C. (in press). Assessing fears in anxiety disordered children with the Revised Fear Survey Schedule for Children (FSSC-R). *Journal of Clinical Child Psychology*.

Last, C. G., Hersen, M., Kazdin, A. E., Finkelstein, R., & Strauss, C. C. (1987). Comparison of DSM-III separation anxiety and overanxious disorders: Demographic characteristics and patterns of comorbidity. *Journal of the American Academy of Child Psychiatry, 26*, 527-531.

Last, C. G., Hersen, M., Kazdin, A. E., Francis, G., & Grubb, H. J. (1987). Psychiatric illness in the mothers of anxious children. *American Journal of Psychiatry, 12*, 1580-1583.

Last, C. G., Hersen, M., & Kazdin, A. E., Orvaschel, H., & Ye, W. (1988). *A family study of childhood anxiety disorders*. Manuscript submitted for publication.

Last, C. G., Phillips, J. E., & Statfeld, A. (1987). Childhood anxiety disorders in mothers and their children. *Child Psychiatry and Human Development, 18*, 103-112.

Leonard, H., Swedo, S., Rapoport, J. L., Coffey, M., & Cheslow, D. (1988). Treatment of childhood obsessive compulsive disorder with clomipramine and desmethylimipramine: A double blind crossover comparison. *Psychopharmacology Bulletin, 24*, 93-95.

Liebowitz, M. R., Fyer, A. J., Gorman, J. M., Campeas, R., & Levin, A. (1986). Phenelzine in social phobia. *Journal of Clinical Psychopharmacology, 6*, 93-98.

Liebowitz, M. R., Gorman, J. M., Fyer, A. J., Campeas, R., Levin, A., Sandberg, D., Hollander, E., Papp, L., & Goetz, D., (1988). Pharmacotherapy of social phobia: A placebo controlled comparison of phenelzine and atenolol. *Journal of Clinical Psychiatry, 49*, 252-257.

Linet, L. S. (1985). Tourette Syndrome, pimozide, and school phobia: The neuroleptic separation anxiety syndrome. *American Journal of Psychiatry, 142*, 613-615.

Livingston, R., Nugent, H., Rader, L., & Smith, G. R. (1985). Family histories of depressed and severely anxious children. *American Journal of Psychiatry, 142*, 1497-1499.

Lorenz, K. Z. (1937). The companion in the bird's world. *Auk., 54*, 245-273.

Malmquist, C. P. (1986). Children who witness parental murder. *Journal of the American Academy of Child Psychiatry, 25*, 320-325.

Mannuzza, S., & Klein, R. (1987). *Schedule for the Assessment of Conduct, Hyperactivity, Anxiety, Mood and Psychoactive Substances (CHAMPS)*. Children's Behavior Disorders Clinic, Long Island Jewish Medical Center, New Hyde Park, NY 11042.

Mansdorf, I. J., & Lukens, E. (1987). Cognitive-behavioral psychotherapy for separation anxious children exhibiting school phobia. *Journal of the American Academy of Child and Adolescent Psychiatry, 26*, 222-225.

Martinez-Monfort, A., & Dreger, R. M. (1972). Reactions of high school students in school desegregation in a Southern metropolitan area. *Psychological Reports, 30*, 543-565.

Mattison, R. E., & Bagnato, S. J. (1987). Empirical measurement of overanxious disorder in boys 8 to 12 years old. *Journal of the American Academy of Child and Adolescent Psychiatry, 26*, 536-540.

Mattison, R. E., Bagnato, S. J., & Brubaker, B. H. (1988). Diagnostic utility of the Revised Children's Manifest Anxiety Scale in children with DSM-III anxiety disorders. *Journal of Anxiety Disorders, 2,* 147-155.

May, R. (1950). *The meaning of anxiety.* New York: Norton.

McReynolds, P. (1978). IPAT Anxiety Scale. In O. K. Buros (Ed.), *The eighth mental measurements yearbook* (p. 859). Lincoln: University of Nebraska.

Miller, L. C. (1967a). Louisville behavior checklist for males, 6-12 years of age. *Psychological Reports, 21,* 885-896.

Miller, L. C. (1967b). Dimensions of psychopathology in middle children. *Psychological Reports, 21,* 897-903.

Miller, L. C., Barrett, C. L., & Hampe, E. (1974). Phobias of childhood in a prescientific era. In A. Davids (Ed.), *Child personality and psychopathology: Current topics.* New York: John Wiley.

Miller, L. C., Barrett, C. L., Hampe, E., & Noble, H. (1971). Revised anxiety scales for the Louisville Behavior Checklist. *Psychological Reports, 29,* 503-511.

Miller, L. C., Barrett, C. L., Hampe, E., & Noble, H. (1972). Comparison of reciprocal inhibition, psychotherapy, and waiting list control for phobic children. *Journal of Abnormal Psychology, 79,* 269-279.

Miller, L. C., Barrett, C. L., Hampe, E., & Noble, H. (1972). Factor structure of childhood fears. *Journal of Consulting and Clinical Psychology, 39,* 264-268.

Miller, L. C., Hampe, E., Barrett, C. L., & Noble, H. (1971). Children's deviant behavior within the general population. *Journal of Consulting and Clinical Psychology, 37,* 16-22.

Mills, H. L., Agras, W. S., Barlow, D. H., & Mills, J. R. (1973). Compulsive rituals treated by response prevention: An experimental analysis. *Archives of General Psychiatry, 338,* 524-529.

Monroe, S. M., & Wade, S. L. (1988). Life Events. In C. G. Last & M. Hersen (Eds.), *Handbook of anxiety disorders.* New York: Pergamon.

Montenegro, H. (1968). Two cases of separation anxiety (preschool) treated with reciprocal inhibition. *Journal of Child Psychology and Psychiatry, 9,* 93-103.

Morris, R. J., & Kratochwill, T. R. (1983). *Treating children's fears and phobias.* New York: Pergamon.

Mowrer, O. H. (1939). Stimulus response theory of anxiety. *Psychological Review, 46,* 553-565.

Mowrer, O. H. (1960). *Learning theory and behavior.* New York: John Wiley.

Ollendick, T. H. (1983). Reliability and validity of the revised Fear Survey Schedule for Children (FSSC-R). *Behaviour Research and Therapy, 21,* 685-692.

Ong, S. B., & Leng, V. K. (1979). The treatment of an obsessive compulsive girl in the context of Malaysian Chinese culture. *Australia and New Zealand Journal of Psychiatry, 13,* 255-259.

Ono, O. (1972). Basic studies of school phobia: An investigation in a local area (Kagawa Prefecture). *Japanese Journal of Child Psychiatry, 13,* 249-260.

Patterson, G. R. (1965). A learning theory approach to the treatment of the school phobic child. In L. Ullmann & L. Krasner (Eds.), *Case studies in behavior modification.* New York: Holt, Rinehart & Winston.

Pauls, D. L., Towbin, K. E., Leckman, J. F., Zahner, E. P., & Cohen, D. J. (1986). Gilles de la Tourette's syndrome and obsessive-compulsive disorder: Evidence supporting a genetic relationship. *Archives of General Psychiatry, 43,* 1180-1182.

Pavlov, I. P. (1941). *Conditioned reflexes and psychiatry.* (W. H. Ganto, Trans.). London: Lawrence and Wishart.

Pecknold, J. D., Swinson, R. P., Kuch, K., & Lewis, C. P. (1988). Alprazolam in panic disorder and agoraphobia: Results from a multicenter trial: Discontinuation effects. *Archives of General Psychiatry, 45,* 429-436.

Perkin, G. J., Rowe, G. P., & Farmer, R. G. (1973). Operant conditioning of emotional responsiveness as a prerequisite for behavioural analysis: A case study of an adolescent school phobic. *Australian and New Zealand Journal of Psychiatry, 7,* 180-183.

Perugi, G., Deltito, J., Soriani, A., Musetti, L., Petracca, A., Nisita, C., Maremmani, I., & Cassano, G. B. (1988). Relationships between panic disorder and separation anxiety with school phobia. *Comprehensive Psychiatry, 29,* 98-107.

Phillips, D., & Wolpe, S. (1981). Multiple behavioral techniques in severe separation anxiety of a twelve-year-old. *Journal of Behavioral and Experimental Psychiatry, 12,* 329-332.

Porter, R. B., & Cattell, R. B. (1979). *The Children's Personality Questionnaire.* Champaign, IL: Institute for Personality and Ability Testing.

Puig-Antich, J., & Chambers, W. J. (1978). Schedule for affective disorders & schizophrenia for school-age children (Present Episode Version) (K-SADS-P). Unpublished manuscript.

Queiroz, L., Motta, M., Madi, M., Sossai, D., & Boren, J. J. (1981). A functional analysis of obsessive-compulsive problems with related therapeutic procedures. *Behavior Research and Therapy, 18,* 377-388.

Rabiner, C. J., & Klein, D. F. (1969). Imipramine treatment of school phobia. *Comprehensive Psychiatry, 10,* 387-390.

Rachman, S. J. (1978). *Fear and courage.* San Francisco: Freeman.

Rank, O. (1952). *The trauma of birth.* New York: Brunner.

Rapoport, J., Elkins, R., & Mikkelsen, E. (1980). Clinical controlled trial of clomipramine in adolescents with obsessive-compulsive disorder. *Psychopharmacology Bulletin, 16,* 61-63.

Reich, W., Herjanic, B., Welner, Z., & Gandhy, P. R. (1982). Development of a structured psychiatric interview for children: Agreement on diagnosis comparing child and parent interviews. *Journal of Abnormal Child Psychology, 10,* 325-336.

Reynolds, C. R. (1980). Concurrent validity of What I Think and Feel: The Revised Children's Manifest Anxiety Scale. *Journal of Consulting and Clinical Psychology, 48,* 774-775.

Reynolds, C. R., & Paget, K. D. (1981). Factor analysis of the Revised Children's Manifest Anxiety Scale for blacks, whites, males, and females with a national normative sample. *Journal of Consulting and Clinical Psychology, 49,* 352-359.

Reynolds, C. R., & Richmond, B. O. (1970). What I Think and Feel: A revised measure of children's manifest anxiety. *Journal of Abnormal Child Psychology, 6,* 271-280.

Reynolds, C. R., & Richmond, B. O. (1979). Factor structure and construct validity of "What I Think and Feel": The revised children's manifest anxiety scale. *Journal of a Personality Assessment, 43,* 281-283.

Reynolds, C. R., & Richmond, B. O. (1984). *Revised Children's Manifest Anxiety Scale.* Los Angeles, CA: Western Psychological Services.

Reznick, J. S., Kagan, J., & Snidman, N. (1986). Inhibited and uninhibited behavior: A follow-up study. *Child Development, 51,* 660-680.

Richman, N., Stevenson, J., & Graham, P. J. (1982). *Preschool to school: A behavioral study.* London: Academic Press.

Roberts, M. (1975). Persistent school refusal among children and adolescents. *Life history research in psychopathology, 4,* 79-198.

Robertson, J., & Bowlby, J. (1952). Observations of the sequences of response of children aged 18 to 24 months during the course of separation. *Courier, 2,* 131-142.

Robins, L. N., Helzer, J. E., Weissman, M. M., Orvaschel, H., Gruenberg, E., Burke, J. D., & Regier, D. (1984). Lifetime prevalence of specific psychiatric disorders in three sites. *Archives of General Psychiatry, 41,* 949-958.

Rodriguez, A., Rodriguez, M., & Eisenberg, L. (1959). The outcome of school phobia: A follow-up study based on 41 cases. *American Journal of Psychiatry, 116,* 540-544.

Rosenbaum, J. F., Biederman, J., Gersten, M., Hirshfield, D. R., Meminger, S. R., Herman, J. B., Kagan, J., Reznick, J. S., & Snidman, N. (1988). Behavioral inhibition in children of parents with panic disorder and agoraphobia. *Archives of General Psychiatry, 45,* 463-470.

Rubinstein, E. A. (1948). Childhood mental disease in America: A review of the literature before 1900. *American Journal of Orthopsychiatry, 18,* 314-320.

Rutter, M. (1976). Research report: Institute of Psychiatry Department of Child and Adolescent Psychiatry. *Psychological Medicine, 6,* 505-516.

Rutter, M., & Graham, P. (1968). The reliability and validity of the psychiatric assessment of the child. I. Interview with the child. *British Journal of Psychiatry, 114,* 563-579.

Rutter, M., Tizard, J., & Whitmore, K. (1981). *Education, health and behaviour.* New York: Krieger.

Sarason, S. B. (1966). The measurement of anxiety in children: Some questions and problems. In C. D. Spielberger (Ed.), *Anxiety and behavior* (pp. 63-79). New York: Academic Press.

Scherer, M. W., & Nakamura, C. Y. (1968). A Fear Survey Schedule for Children (FSS-FC): A factor analytic comparison with manifest anxiety (CMAS). *Behaviour Research and Therapy, 6,* 173-182.

Seligman, M. (1970). On the generality of the laws of learning. *Psychological Review, 77,* 406-418.

Shaffer, D., Schonfeld, I., O'Connor, P. A., Stokman, C., Trautman, P., Shafer, S., and Ng, S. (1985). Neurological soft signs: Their relationship to psychiatric disorder and intelligence in childhood and adolescence. *Archives of General Psychiatry, 42,* 342-351.

Shaffer, D., Schwab-Stone, M., Fisher, P., Davies, M., Piacentini, J., & Gioia, P. (1988). A revised version of the Diagnostic Interview Schedule for Children (DISC-R). Unpublished manuscript.

Sherman, M. (1927). The differentiation of emotional responses in infants. *Journal of Comparative Psychology, 7,* 265-284, 335-351.

Silverman, W. K., & Nelles, W. B. (1988). The anxiety disorders interview schedule for children. *Journal of the American Academy of Child and Adolescent Psychiatry, 27,* 772-778.

Simeon, J. G., & Ferguson, H. B. (1985). Recent developments in the use of antidepressants and anxiolytics. *The Psychiatric Clinics of North America, 8* (4).

Simeon, J. G., & Ferguson, H. B. (1987). Alprazolam effects in children with anxiety disorders. *Canadian Journal of Psychiatry, 32,* 570-574.

Smith, S. L. (1970). School refusal with anxiety; A review of sixty-three cases. *Canadian Psychiatric Association Journal, 126,* 815-817.

Smith, R. E., & Sharpe, T. M. (1970). Treatment of a school phobia with implosive therapy. *Journal of Consulting and Clinical Psychology, 35,* 239-243.

Spielberger, C. D. (1973). *State-Trait Anxiety Inventory for Children.* Palo Alto, CA: Consulting Psychologists Press.

Spitzer, R. L., Williams, J. B. W., & Gibbon, M. (1986). Structured clinical interviews for DSM-III-R. Unpublished manuscript.

Stanley, L. (1980). Treatment of ritualistic behavior in an eight-year-old girl by response prevention: A case report. *Journal of Child Psychology and Psychiatry, 21,* 85-90.

Strauss, C. C., Last, C. G., Hersen, M., & Kazdin, A. E. (1988). Association between anxiety and depression in children and adolescents with anxiety disorders. *Journal of Abnormal Child Psychology, 16,* 57-68.

Strauss, C. C., Lease, C. A., Last, C. G., & Francis, G. (1988). Overanxious disorder: An examination of development differences. *Journal of Abnormal Child Psychology, 16,* 433-443.

Strober, M., Green, J., & Carlson, G. (1981). Reliability of psychiatric diagnosis in hospitalized adolescents. *Archives of General Psychiatry, 38,* 141-145.

Sullivan, H. D. (1956). *Clinical Studies in Psychiatry.* New York: W. W. Norton.

Sulloway, F. L. (1979). *Freud: Biologist of the Mind.* New York: Basic Books.

Suomi, S. J., Seaman, S. F., Lewis, J. K., DeLizio, R. D., & McKinney, W. T. (1978). Effects of imipramine treatment of separation-induced social disorders in Rhesus monkeys. *Archives of General Psychiatry, 35,* 321-327.

Swedo, S. E., & Rapoport, J. L. (1989). Phenomenology and differential diagnosis of obsessive-compulsive disorder in children and adolescents. In J. L. Rapoport (Ed.), *Obsessive Compulsive Disorder in Children and Adolescents* (pp. 13-32). Washington, DC: American Psychiatric Press.

Sylvester, C. E., Hyde, T. S., & Reichler, R. J. (1987). The Diagnostic Interview for Children and Personality Inventory for Children in studies of children at risk for anxiety disorders or depression. *Journal of the American Academy of Child and Adolescent Psychiatry, 26,* 668-675.

Terr, L. C. (1981). Psychic trauma in children: Observations following the Chowchilla school bus kidnapping. *American Journal of Psychiatry, 138,* 14-19.

Thomas, A., Chess, S., Birch, H. G., Hertzig, M., & Korn, S. J. (1963). *Behavioral individuality in early childhood.* New York: University Press.

Thoren, P., Asberg, M., Cronholm, B., Jornestedt, H., & Traskman, L. (1980). Clomipramine treatment of obsessive-compulsive disorder. I. A controlled clinical trial. *Archives of General Psychiatry, 37,* 1281-1285.

Thorndike, R. L. (1978). Critique. In O. K. Buros (Ed.), *The eighth mental measurements yearbook* (p. 766). Lincoln: University of Nebraska.

Thorpe, L. P., Clark, W. W., & Tiegs, E. W. (1953a). *California test of personality. Primary form.* Monterey, CA: McGraw-Hill.

Thorpe, L. P., Clark, W. W., & Tiegs, E. W. (1953b). *California test of personality. Elementary form.* Monterey, CA: McGraw-Hill.

Tiegs, E. W., Clark, W. W., & Thorpe, L. P. (1953). *California test of personality. Secondary form.* Monterey, CA: McGraw-Hill.

Tinbergen, N. (1958). *Curious naturalists.* New York: Doubleday.

Torgerson, S. (1988). Genetics. In C. G. Last, & M. Hersen (Eds.), *Handbook of anxiety disorders.* New York: Pergamon.

Trueman, D. (1984). What are the characteristics of school phobic children? *Psychological Reports, 54,* 191-202.

Turner, S. M., Beidel, D. C., & Costello, A. (1987). Psychopathology in the offspring of anxiety disorders patients. *Journal of Consulting and Clinical Psychology, 55,* 229-235.

Vaal, J. J. (1973). Applying contingency contracting to a school phobic: A case study. *Journal of Behavior Therapy and Experimental Psychiatry, 4,* 371-737.

Valentine, C. W. (1946). *The Psychology of Early Childhood* (3rd ed.) London: Methuen.

van der Ploeg-Stapert, J. D. & van der Ploeg, H. M. (1986). Behavioral group treatment of test anxiety; An evaluation study. *Journal of Behavior Therapy and Experimental Psychiatry, 17,* 255-259.

Waldron, S. (1976). The significance of childhood neurosis for adult mental health: A follow-up study. *American Journal of Psychiatry, 133,* 532-538.

Walk, A. (1964). The pre-history of child psychiatry. *British Journal of Psychiatry, 110,* 754-767.

Warren, W. (1965). A study of adolescent psychiatric inpatients and the outcome six or more years later. I. Clinical histories and hospital findings. *Journal of Child Psychology and Psychiatry, 6,* 1-17.

Watson, J. (1924). *Behaviorism.* New York: W. W. Norton.

Watson, J., & Rayner, R. (1920). Conditioned emotional reactions. *Journal of Experimental Psychology, 3,* 1-22.

Weiss, M. & Burke, A. (1970). A 5- to 10-year follow-up of hospitalized school phobic children and adolescents. *American Journal of Orthopsychiatry, 40,* 672-676.

Weissman, M. M. (in press). Evidence for comorbidity for anxiety and depression: Family and genetic studies of children. In J. D. Maser & C. R. Cloninger (Eds.), *Co-morbidity of mood & anxiety disorders.* Washington, DC: American Psychiatric Press.

Weissman, M. M., Leckman, J. R., Merikangas, K. R., Gammon, G. D., & Prusoff, B. A. (1984). Depression and anxiety disorders in parents and children: Results from the Yale Family Study. *Archives of General Psychiatry, 41,* 845-852.

Welch, M. W., & Carpenter, C. (1970). Solution of a school phobia contingency contracting. *School Applications of Learning Theory, 2,* 11-17.

Williams, J. M. G., Murray, J. J., Lund, C. A., Harkiss, B., & DeFranco, A. (1985). Anxiety in the child dental clinic. *Journal of Child Psychology and Psychiatry, 26,* 305-310.

Wirt, R. D., Lachar, D., Klinedinst, J. K., & Seat, P. D. (1977). *Multidimensional description of child personality: A manual for the personality inventory for children.* Los Angeles: Western Psychological Services.

Wise, S. P., & Rapoport, J. L. (1989). Obsessive-compulsive disorder: Is it basal ganglia dysfunction? In J. L. Rapoport (Ed.), *Obsessive-compulsive disorder in children and adolescents* (pp. 327-344). Washington, DC: American Psychiatric Press.

Wisniewski, J. J., Mulick, J. A., Genshaft, J. L., & Coury, D. L. (1987). Test-retest reliability of the Revised Children's Manifest Anxiety Scale. *Perceptual and Motor Skills, 65,* 67-70.

Wolpe, J., & Lang, P. J. (1964). A fear survey schedule for use in behavior therapy. *Behavior Research and Therapy, 2,* 27-30.

Wolpe, J., & Rachman, S. (1960). Psychoanalytic evidence: A critique based on Freud's case of Little Hans. *Journal of Nervous and Mental Diseases, 131,* 135-145.

Zikis, P. (1983). Treatments of an 11-year-old ritualizer and tiquer girl with in vivo exposure and response prevention. *Behavioral Psychology, 11,* 75-81.

Zitrin, C. M., Klein, D. F., Woerner, M. G., & Ross, D. C. (1983). Treatment of phobias: I. Comparison of imipramine hydrochloride and placebo. *Archives of General Psychiatry, 40,* 125-138.

Ziv, A., & Israeli, R. (1973). Effects of bombardment on the manifest anxiety level of children living in kibbutzim. *Journal of Consulting and Clinical Psychology, 40,* 287-291.

INDEX

Abusive parents, and attachment behaviors, 24
Adolescents
    conduct disorder in, 108
    separation anxiety disorder in, 32
    (*See also* Childhood anxiety disorders)
Adult psychopathology, and childhood anxiety disorders, 104-119
Age
    avoidant disorder and, 39
    obsessive-compulsive disorder and, 39
    overanxious disorder and, 38
    separation anxiety disorder and, 38
Aggression, Freudian theory of, 14
Agoraphobia
    classification, 29-30
    separation anxiety disorder and, 77, 106, 115, 117-118
    panic disorder and, 31, 86
    school phobias and, 117-118
Aloneness, and separation anxiety, 29, 33
Alprazolam (Xanax)
    overanxious disorder and, 80-81
    separation anxiety disorder and, 79-80
Animal experiments, inducing fears in, 20
Annihilation, fear of, 17
Antihistamines, treating anxiety with, 76
Anxiety
    age-adequate mastery of, 16
    assessment of, 44-46
    as trait, 46
    attachment and, 22-25
    conditioning theory, 19-21
    depressive disorders and, 13, 105
    ethological theories, 22
    fear and, 22
    Freudian concepts, 13-17
    learning theory, 19-20
    Neo-Freudian concepts, 18
    normal, 24

subjective, 45
symptoms, 42
    (*See also* Anxiety disorders; Childhood anxiety disorders)
Anxiety disorders
    depression and, 85-86
    follow-up studies, 107-115
    generalized, 31, 97
    hereditary influences, 21, 93-97
    lifetime history, 91
    stress and, 34, 38, 98-99
    (*See also* Anxiety; Childhood anxiety disorders)
Anxiety Disorders Interview Schedule for Children (ADIS), 61
Anxiety scales
    consistency in, 53
    children's self-rating, 46-54
    parents' assessment, 55-60
Anxiolytics, 77, 80
Apathy, and separation anxiety, 29, 33
Assertiveness, Freudian theory of, 16
Assessment, of anxiety, 44-66
    self-rating scales, 46-54
    parent scales, 55-60
    personality tests, 44-46
    psychological tests, 61
    structured diagnostic interviews, 60-61
Attachment behaviors
    abuse and, 24
    classification, 29
    development and, 22-25
    natural selection and, 23
Attention deficit hyperactivity disorder (ADHD), 65, 91-92
Avoidant disorder
    behavioral treatment, 72
    classification, 29-30
    diagnosis, 37-39
    overanxious disorder and, 37

ABOUT THE AUTHORS

RACHEL G. KLEIN, Ph.D., is Professor of Clinical Psychology (in Psychiatry) at Columbia University, College of Physicians and Surgeons, and Director of Psychology at the New York State Psychiatric Institute and the Columbia Presbyterian Medical Center. She has been an active investigator in the field of childhood psychopathology for nearly 2 decades. She has been the recipient of grant awards from the NIMH to investigate the treatment as well as the natural history of childhood and adolescent psychopathology. Dr. Klein has published numerous scientific papers in child psychopathology and has conducted a number of studies in the field of childhood anxiety. She is coauthor (with Donald F. Klein, Frederic Quitkin, and Arthur Rifkin) of a standard textbook in psychiatric diagnosis treatment, *Diagnosis and drug treatment of psychiatric disorders: Adults and children,* (Williams & Wilkins). Dr. Klein played a major role in the formulation of the DSM-III classification of childhood disorders and is the editor of the only previous volume on childhood anxiety disorder, *Anxiety disorders of childhood* (Guilford Press).

CYNTHIA G. LAST, Ph.D., is Associate Professor of Psychiatry and Director of the Child and Adolescent Anxiety Disorder Clinic at Western Psychiatric Institute and Clinic, University of Pittsburgh School of Medicine. Dr. Last's clinical research focuses on the assessment, diagnosis, and treatment of childhood anxiety disorders, and she has received several research grants from the National Institute of Mental Health to study these issues in anxiety disordered children. Dr. Last has published numerous scientific papers and books chapters in the area of anxiety disorders, and is editor of seven books, including *Handbook of anxiety disorder,* (coedited with Michel Hersen, Pergamon Press) and the forthcoming *Anxiety across the lifespan: A developmental perspective on anxiety and the anxiety disorders* (Springer Publications). She is also editor and founder of the *Journal of Anxiety Disorders.*

NOTES

NOTES

NOTES

NOTES